12 AT WAR

Great Photographers Under Fire

Twelve great photographers are portrayed at work recording man's numerous wars. Here is Mathew Brady following the battles of the Civil War, and the pioneer before him, Fenton at the Crimean War; here, too, are contemporary photographers such as Margaret Bourke-White and David Douglas Duncan; and the legendary Robert Capa, one of many war photographers who died plying his trade. The story of each is accompanied with several of his photographs. Author Robert E. Hood is the editor of *Boys' Life* magazine.

This famous photograph caught a Spanish Loyalist at the moment of his death. (Photo by Robert Capa, Images of War, copyright 1964)

12 AT WAR

Great Photographers Under Fire

by Robert E. Hood

G. P. Putnam's Sons   New York, New York

For Carol and Eric, to show them integrity and courage in action

CONTENTS

Acknowledgments

Dozens and dozens of cameramen, photographic specialists and just plain photo buffs were consulted in the course of writing this book. My sincere thanks to all who helped me, even though it is impractical to list each of you here. I am particularly indebted and grateful to Margaret Bourke-White, Edward Steichen, Carl Mydans, David Duncan, Henri Cartier-Bresson and André Kertesz, who answered difficult questions about war photography and their role in it with great patience and thoughtfulness. Special thanks go to Cornell Capa for providing insight and information in depth about his brother, Bob; and to Mrs. Eileen Shneiderman, who was equally kind and insightful about her brother, David Seymour. John Faber, historian of the National Press Photographers Association, deserves special thanks, too, for sharing his voluminous knowledge and personal library. My apologies to all the fine war photographers excluded from this book by space limitations. There are more than enough of you to make another volume or two; your stories are well worth telling, and perhaps will be told someday.

The Dangerous Profession

ERNEST HEMINGWAY called war the "sad science." To General Karl von Clausewitz, the brilliant German militarist of the nineteenth century, it was "only a continuation of State policy by other means." For photographer Robert Capa war was "like an aging actress, more and more dangerous and less and less photogenic."

No matter how one describes war—call it pure hell or human malignancy on a global scale—it lingers on, century after century, despite conferences and pacts and treaties, from League of Nations to United Nations. Violence has had its own continuity—and a terrifying one—from the pass at Thermopylae to the rice paddies in Vietnam. The threat has always hovered, whether shaped like a spear or a monstrous mushroom: the record has been clear and continuous.

The simple fact that war exists—like a dangerous mountain beyond the horizon or a partly submerged iceberg—means it cannot be ignored: it has to be recorded; events must be reported; brave deeds praised. The grim irony is that death and devastation, triumph and tragedy make war a dramatic subject for the reporter, whether he uses a pencil, a brush or camera. Men in pain and under great stress, women and children fearful and in agony, patrols moving forward, planes and helicopters overhead— for me the face of war is most stark in the works of fine photographers, famous and unknown alike. The brilliant photos of David Douglas Duncan, the powerful images of Capa; the strong point of view of Margaret Bourke-White, Carl Mydans and Eugene Smith; the dozens of great pictures taken by photographers long since forgotten, some of whom worked for the Armed Forces and remain anonymously—and sadly—just,

"Signal Corps." They have all contributed to a tapestry of images that stretches back more than a hundred years.

Up until the nineteenth century the role of war reporter was played by writers or painters, some obscure or nameless, others with the renown of Thucydides or Goya. With the invention of a workable camera, there was a fresh way to record violence, and a fresh scorekeeper ventured onto the scene.

In 1855, Roger Fenton, an Englishman, sailed from England, bound for Balaklava to photograph the Crimean War. His equipment was crude and cumbersome but he returned to London with a collection of negatives, mostly portraits of men and scenic battlefields, but no views of action or destruction. Fenton was the first successful war photographer,* but the American who followed him is revered by most people as the founding father of this grim profession.

Every profession tends to sanctify its precursors, often justifiably so, as in the case of Mathew B. Brady, who was the leading portrait photographer in America and a wealthy man when Civil War broke out. Brady conceived the idea of making a complete record of war (and, to a remarkable extent, Edward Steichen followed in his footsteps in World War II). He was not only a fine photographer himself but an amazing organizer, who invested $100,000 to outfit and train war photographers. At times he had fifty wagons in the field, rolling darkrooms and supply vehicles. He was the photographic news bureau of his day, and the result of his logistical genius was an almost comprehensive picture of war. For this great labor of love, Brady, at war's end, was nearly a financial wreck, but he anticipated the government and people would reward him for his great service so he could recoup his losses. Sad to say, no one was very interested in his gallery, and in 1896 Mathew B. Brady died, neglected, in the poor ward of a New York hospital.

History has vindicated Brady. And the bushy-haired little Irishman left war photographers a personal legacy which they still draw on: a

---

* He is usually credited as being the "first war photographer," but this is not literally true. According to Helmut Gernsheim in *The History of Photography* (London, 1955), that title belongs to Karl Baptist Von Szathmari. An amateur photographer who lived in Bucharest, he photographed Russian generals and camp scenes after war broke out in Wallachia in November of 1853. Later, he covered the Turks, following the fighting in the Danube valley.

Turkish troops about to sail from Braila, Rumania, in 1918. (By André Kertesz)

passion for documentation, a sense of history and high artistic standards.

The photographer belongs in the community of artists alongside the writer and painter; all three have shown their fellow citizens the futility of war, and, at the highest level, their spiritual brotherhood is a tradition of courage and compassion. One thinks quickly of Tolstoy's massive *War and Peace*; of Stendhal's personalistic view of Waterloo in *The Charterhouse of Parma*; of Goya's sketches in *The Disasters of War* or Luis Quintanilla's drawings of the Spanish Civil War, *All the Brave*; of Robert Capa's *Images of War*. The camera, the pen, the brush—these are only tools. The essential qualities and qualifications are power of observation, an understanding of military tactics and strategy, an ability to impose order on chaos, a fine sensibility and a sensitivity to suffering, an honest point of view and an active conscience.

War is risky; the very qualities that make an artist lessen his possibility of success and of survival in battle. Apprehension is the enemy of courage, imagination is a perpetual threat. The photographer is especially susceptible, for he must function coolly in a cauldron of bullets and bombs, of smoke and dust.

The strength of photography lies in its on-the-spot reality, and no prose or painting can compete with this immediacy. To do his job the photographer ventures through an explosive landscape, risking his life as a matter of course. Some take incredible risks, as though challenging death itself. For example, Kyoichi Sawada, who won the Pulitzer Prize in 1966, was reprimanded in Vietnam for running through a field of booby traps *ahead* of the troops.

A writer or painter can store up literary or pictorial images, later to be placed on page or canvas; he can sit in the rear lines sifting reports or view battle from a distance and still make a significant contribution to history. The photographer cannot, nor does he have much time for contemplation, owing to the fleeting nature of photography. Besides this, he is at the mercy of a mechanical process, which makes for continual anxiety: if his equipment fails—if his camera falls into water or a shutter freezes—he has failed.

Just as there are all kinds of human beings, so there are all kinds of war photographers, with a variety of motives, from the noble "protestor"

10

to the glory-seeker to the guy who is there simply to do a job. With a variety of skills and sensibilities at work, a tremendous range and sweep of images results—and a photograph taken for one purpose may wind up serving quite a different end. A simple "record" shot might later be used for propaganda or as a recruiting poster.

At the highest level of conscience—the level of art—the communicator —writer, painter, photographer—is aware of the perniciousness of war. But even the best-intentioned, strongest antiwar statements have little deterrent effect, or at least haven't up to our time. Stephen Crane's *The Red Badge of Courage*, Erich Maria Remarque's *All Quiet on the Western Front*, Hemingway's *A Farewell to Arms*, Picasso's *Guernica*, Brady and Gardner's Civil War photos—all these made only momentary shock waves. Alas, at best, the artist is only a gadfly, who periodically stings us into awareness.

Of course, there have been various kinds of wars, some of which had to be fought, to liberate oppressed people and to preserve freedom and human dignity. War is always atrocious, but in a just cause the camera may advance victory, serving as a useful tool for reconnaissance and espionage, not to mention its value as a means of propaganda. But a photographer must pause nowadays before using his talent to promote or glorify war; the hydrogen bomb lurks beyond the next hill and the concept of "limited war" is semantic. War in the twentieth century is much more than soldiers blowing one another to bits, as you will see in the photographic folios that follow. It is lines of refugees tramping the roads and clogging the bridges of Europe and Asia; it is despair looking through barbed wire; it is children playing in rubble and poking through garbage cans in search of lunch. It is massive and all-inclusive.

As long as there are West Points in the world turning out strategists, munitions makers turning out arms and bands playing military airs, there is a possibility of war.

But it may very well be that the photographer who made the greatest single contribution to mankind was the one who took the first clear exposure of that awful mushroom cloud.

No matter how large—or how slight—the impact of a war photograph, the man behind the image deserves respect and praise, and his work ought to be remembered. Who recalls the intrepid Jimmy Hare, the pioneer aerial photographer, who covered the Spanish-American War, the Russo-Japanese War, the Balkan War and World War I? Who has seen the rare World War I photos of André Kertesz, who is the father of candid war photography?

That is why I set out years ago to interview photographers, to write to them and to their friends and, when possible, to speak to them directly, by telephone or face to face. A surprising number answered my questionnaire, although most preferred to sit down and chat. Most photojournalists do not leave written records; their constant preoccupation with the visual world, their style of life—they are perpetual vagabonds—makes writing arduous and painful. The exceptions are visual-verbal people—the switch-hitters of the communications world—such as Bourke-White, David Duncan, and Carl Mydans.

This is a book about photographers as human beings and artists, attempting to show what they are like, the contributions they made, and how war affected them. And, to paraphrase Mark Twain's Notice to *Huckleberry Finn*: Persons attempting to classify this narrative as a history of combat photography will be prosecuted; persons looking forward to a handbook of atrocities will be banished; persons searching for information about cameras, film, lights, etc., will be shot. (It would take several volumes—and several decades of research—to tell the complete story of war photography. Perhaps someone will do it someday; the material is there, if a writer has the stamina to research it.)

War is grim and dark, but it has many moments both light and touching, as you will discover in the lives of several of these great people. I hope that you will find some of these chapters meaningful, and discover that certain old-fashioned values—courage, devotion and integrity, for example—still play vital roles in the lives of people.

SECTION I
PIONEERS

Roger Fenton posed for his picture before swinging into action.

Roger Fenton

Before the battle, things looked pastoral in this shot taken during the Crimean War. (By Roger Fenton, from the collection of the Library of Congress)

1. At Balaklava

HEAT COVERED the field like a shroud and the hooves of horses filled the air with dust. Inside the darkroom on wheels the temperature was sizzling. The developing water nearly scalded the hands that dipped into it. But the photographer toiled on, sweat pouring down his face, stopping now and then to wipe his brow and listen to the artillery fire thundering in the distance.

It was the summer of 1855 and the Crimean War thundered over Balaklava, Russia—the scene of the "Charge of the Light Brigade" and the place where Florence Nightingale won renown. The Englishman Roger Fenton and his assistant, Marcus Sparling, a former corporal, inventor, and author of a textbook on photography. They were making the

first detailed documentation of war ever attempted in the history of photography. There had been daguerreotypes taken during the Mexican War—by an unknown cameraman—but these showed only officers and men and no sign of combat. Fenton was photographing the actual field of battle, under fire. It was a hazardous and incredibly difficult feat, requiring courage, stamina and dedication:

"I don't think," he wrote in a letter, "if I could have foreseen all the difficulties of my task before setting out, that I should have had the courage to come, but by pitching into them one by one, I suppose they will be mastered."

Merely moving the van from place to place was laborious and danger-

Cannonballs litter the road into the "valley of the shadow of death," a field made famous in Tennyson's poem "The Charge of the Light Brigade."

ous. Great distances and tough terrain had to be covered to get to the lines. The countryside was barren and bleak and the photo van could be seen for miles, a clear target for Russian artillerymen who may have thought it was an ammunition wagon. The equipment was awkward and heavy: five cameras, seven hundred glass plates, chemicals, in addition to a tent, tools, utensils, tinned food, harnesses—in all, thirty-six large cases of equipment!

The developing of the wet plates in the collodion process was a nightmarish experience in the excessive heat of the covered wagon. They required careful handling, skillful and speedy work, and a single mistake in the seven-step process spelled failure. Fenton and his assistant had to clean and polish the glass and coat it with collodion and other chemicals to get a tough, skinlike film. Then the plate, still sticky, was taken into the darkroom and made sensitive to light by soaking in silver nitrate for five minutes. When it turned yellow, it was removed, drained when still wet, and placed in a lightproof holder.

After exposure, the plate had to be rushed back into the darkroom and treated with additional chemicals. When the image was fully developed, the plate had to be rinsed in clear water; then the photographer had to fan it over a light flame to dry it. After which, he varnished it.

This marathon process took place in the heat of battle, with shells whistling overhead. Once an enemy shell ripped a section of roof from the Fenton van, and this had to be repaired immediately. But the most onerous demand made on Fenton was the constant request that he take portraits of people: "If I refuse to take them," he complained, "I get no facilities for conveying my van from one locality to another."

Still, Fenton managed to return to London with more than three hundred negatives, which later were exhibited in London and Paris. Wood engravings were made of some of the scenes, and printed in the *Illustrated London News*. There were no action pictures, for the camera of that day was incapable of capturing them. But there were battlefields, forts, landscapes and portraits of the troops. Fenton had put on film the authenticity of war in a way the public had never seen before.

This was the first war covered in the contemporary style, on-the-scene reportage by writers, artists and photographers. Sir William Howard Russell wrote articles on the action for the *Times* of London; his dispatches and Fenton's photographs brought the war home to the people of England. Although Roger Fenton went to the Crimea on his own, his expedition seems to have been backed by the government and by Thomas Agnew, the Manchester publisher. Fenton carried letters of introduction from Prince Albert to important dignitaries and military commanders, who treated him as a very important person. His photographic coverage was followed up by James Robertson, an amateur photographer and at the time chief engraver to the Imperial Mint in Constantinople. Robertson photographed the fall of Sebastopol, taking some excellent shots of English and French entrenchments and of Russian batteries.

Roger Fenton, like Mathew Brady, was already an accomplished photographer before he ventured onto the battlefield. He was well-known for his portraits, scenics and architectural photographs. He was the first secretary of the Photographic Society of London, and had studied painting in Paris. Photographs of Fenton at Balaklava show a bearded, pipe-smoking man cradling a rifle in his arm. And sitting on the seat of his photo van he looks solid and grim with determination.

Determined, courageous—he proved to be both in the heat and dust of Balaklava.

Photo taken
July 22nd
1861

BRADY
The Photographer
returned from
Bull Run

Mathew Brady

After Appomattox in 1865, Mathew Brady photographed General Robert E. Lee, his son, and a staff officer on the back porch of the Lee house in Richmond, Virginia. (Civil War photos reproduced from the collections of the Library of Congress)

*Above: Officers of 1st Connecticut Artillery, at Fort Brady. Below: Union soldiers
relaxing at gun emplacement. (Photos by Brady or assistant)*

2. Mathew Brady: The Eye of History

THERE IS AN elusive quality to Mathew Brady, as though the massive authenticity of his work had shoved him into the shadows. He left no journal or memoirs of his experiences—not even a single handwritten note—and to this day there is doubt that the grand little genius could even write his own name, let alone keep a diary! Facts on his background and marriage are meager and confusing, even his birthdate and birthplace cannot be given with any degree of exactness. He has been misunderstood by unsympathetic people who failed to appreciate his accomplishments; he was ignored, neglected and treated in a downright shabby fashion by an ungrateful government. Despite an early career of fame and considerable affluence, he died in penniless obscurity. Yet he may have been the greatest photographer America has ever produced. Like most visual titans, the true barometer of his worth— and of his indomitable character—lies in the images he left to posterity.

He had a pointed beard and a big nose, and his eyes grew so weak he could scarcely see, even through spectacles with heavy lenses. He went to war dressed in a broadcloth suit, a long linen duster and a straw hat. After the battle of Bull Run, he returned to his Washington studio, his duster soiled and wrinkled, carrying a sword given to him by some Zouaves who had found him in the woods where he had been lost for three days. He had been shot at and nearly killed; he was hungry and weary; he had lost all his photographic equipment and his van, which soldiers called the "what-is-it?" wagon. He promptly bought new equipment, organized his assistants and hurried back to war. For he was obsessed with the dream that he could do what never had been done before—provide a thorough photographic documentation of war.

Years later, in a newspaper interview in 1891, he explained his passion to record the war even though it cost him his personal fortune and nearly his life: "I can only describe the destiny that overruled me by saying that, like Euphorion, I felt that I had to go. A spirit in my feet said, 'go' and I went. . . ."

Mathew B. Brady was a famous, prosperous photographer long before the Civil War. Known as "Brady of Broadway," he counted among his clientele distinguished Americans, celebrated politicians, soldiers, actors, scientists and writers. Abraham Lincoln said of him: "Brady and the Cooper Institute made me President of the United States." He made numerous photographs of life in the America of his day—of buildings, parades, public functions and the like. In 1850, Mathew Brady brought out a book he had long dreamed of, his *Gallery of Illustrious Americans*. Bound in thick brown covers, the title etched in gold, it weighed five pounds. In it were "portraits of twelve of the most eminent citizens of the American Republic since the days of Washington, all from the original daguerreotypes by Brady." It sold for thirty dollars, was an artistic success but a financial failure. But this project points to Brady's concern with posterity and his role as a photographic historian—a role he would round out during the Civil War.

Who was this determined little man with the large sense of history and of his role in it? Where did he come from? What was he really like?

In his fine biography *Mathew Brady, Historian With a Camera*, James D. Horan grapples with these questions and others. Brady's early years were "shadowy," the biographer points out. He was born "about 1823–24," Brady told an interviewer many years later, in Warren County, near Lake George, New York. Nothing is known about his parents, who probably were Irish immigrants. In those days Warren County was still a frontier, and young Brady left there as a teenager for Saratoga, according to biographer Horan, "the mecca of the farm lads who sought jobs in the outside world." There he teamed up with a young artist, William Page, who encouraged him to sketch. The two young men traveled together, Brady copying sketches, Page looking for portrait commissions.

Sometime in 1839 or 1840 Brady and Page left Albany, where they had been working, for New York City. Page opened a studio and Brady got a job as a clerk in a store. Page introduced Brady to Samuel F. B. Morse, inventor of the telegraph and pioneer in a new, fascinating medium, photography. To Morse, the brand-new technique of the daguerreotype—invented by the Frenchman Daguerre, whom he had met —was a bread-and-butter proposition. Around 1840, Morse started a school of photography, perhaps the first one opened in the United States. Among his students was young Mathew B. Brady, the bushy-haired boy from Warren County. To raise the fifty dollars Morse charged for his course—a large sum at that time—Brady had to work days as a clerk and nights in a small shop. From 1841 until 1843, nobody knows for sure what Brady was doing. He may still have been a clerk and still going to photography school. It is known that he was a member of the early group of daguerreotypists who made New York a mecca for the new profession.

In 1844, Mathew Brady opened his own studio on Fulton Street at Broadway. For the next few years he worked from dawn until dark taking pictures, and throughout most of the night developing them. A shy man, precise and perfectionistic, he worked so intensely that he ruined his eyes, which were weak to begin with. But his talent, great energy and the will to prosper made him a successful portrait photographer. He began his grandiose project to photograph great Americans, starting with former President Andrew Jackson, and in 1849 he captured on film Zachary Taylor and his Cabinet. A year later, he photographed Henry Clay, John Calhoun and Daniel Webster. Brady kept adding to his fame and, although devoted to photography, found time to marry the lovely young Julia Handy. The exact date of the marriage—like other facts in Brady's background—is not known, but the marriage was happy though childless.

Early in his life Brady somehow developed a sense of history, and it kept growing and growing until it seemed literally to burst when Civil War struck America. And from that day on it dominated his thinking, to the exclusion of everything else.

Like all great portraitists, Mathew Brady had a way with people. Although he was reticent and seems to have been reserved, he had the knack of the Irishman to tell a story and relax a subject before his lens. When he was determined to put a man or woman on film, he was relentless in pursuit. After the surrender at Appomattox Courthouse, which he missed due to faulty communications, Brady pursued Robert E. Lee to Richmond. With the help of Lee's wife, he convinced the sad, dispirited general to sit for a portrait, in the interest of history. "Of course," Brady said later in an interview, "I had known him since the Mexican War when he was upon General Scott's staff and my request was not as an intruder."

Brady used every trick and pulled every string available when he decided to document the war. He was a friend of General Winfield Scott, commander of the Union forces in 1861. He hurried to Washington from his New York studio, making his request in person to the aging general. Scott told him that he was about to be replaced by General McDowell and that the photographer would have to see his successor. Instead, after war was declared, he went directly to the White House and put his case to Allan Pinkerton, the famous detective, and President Abraham Lincoln. When Pinkerton agreed to the proposal, Lincoln wrote his approval on a piece of paper: "Pass Brady."

The photographer knew that he would have to finance the entire project out of his own pocket, for Lincoln warned him that the federal government would not contribute a nickel. He knew the undertaking would be expensive and extremely dangerous, yet he could not wait to begin.

Mathew Brady and his assistants went to war in plain old delivery wagons, closed in to make darkrooms and with places for sleeping quarters. They were awkward conveyances, filled with fragile glass plates and cameras, and had to navigate muddy or rutted country roads, depending on the season. They were difficult to maneuver in the swirl of battle, among charging horses and milling troops. At Bull Run, in July, 1861, Union troops stampeded in mad retreat, flinging their rifles aside and running for their lives. Shells burst on the road, horses bolted, wagons were overturned in a crazy jumble of men and animals and equipment. Brady's "What-is-it?" wagon was upended, scattering his precious plates in the smoke and dust of defeat. But the indomitable photographer managed to salvage a few of his wet plates in their wooden boxes, took to the woods, and wandered around until rescued. Back in his Washington studio, he posed for his own picture, a quaint character in a long coat, wearing a bow tie and straw hat!

The Bull Run photos had a big sale and made an immediate impression on the nation's press. *Humphrey's Journal* printed an essay of praise:

> The public is indebted to Brady of Broadway for numerous excellent views of "grim-visaged war." He has been in Virginia with his camera, and many and spirited are the pictures he has taken. His are the only reliable records at Bull's Run. . . .
>
> Brady has shown more pluck than many officers and soldiers who were in the fight. He went—not exactly like the "Sixty-Ninth," stripped to the pants—but with his sleeves tucked up and his big camera directed upon every point of interest in the field. . . .
>
> The groupings of entire regiments and divisions, within a space of a couple of feet square, present some of the most curious effects as yet produced in photography. Considering the circumstances under which they were taken, amidst the excitement, the rapid movements, and the smoke of the battlefield, there is nothing to compare with them in their powerful contrasts of light and shade.

After Bull Run, Mathew Brady began lining up the photographic task force that would cover almost every combat arena, traveling with the Armies of the Potomac, Cumberland, Tennessee, Red River and the Gulf. He became, in effect, the first photographic agency specializing in war photography. It would cost him a fortune in savings, not to mention commissions he might have earned from commercial portraits; he would neglect his business, worry his wife and friends, and risk death on various occasions. Yet without his single-mindedness we would not have the treasury of Civil War images. Photography would not have been so quickly and brilliantly recognized as a superb means of documentation. And two of his famous assistants—Alexander Gardner, who later published his own two volumes, *Sketchbook of the Civil War*, and Timothy O'Sullivan, who went on to do brilliant postwar photography—might never have reached their potential.

As an entrepreneur and businessman, Brady copyrighted all photographs in his name. His investment made the project possible and his name, a household word in the nation, helped sell the pictures. So he undoubtedly felt justified in stamping "photograph by Brady" on all staff work, although this practice must have galled his assistants, and has led to the modern charge that he made few of the Civil War photos credited to him. Obviously, it would have been impossible for him to have made the great documentation with his own hands. Alexander Gardner and Tim O'Sullivan took many of the pictures. According to James Horan's biography of Brady, Gardner took seventy-five percent of the coverage of the Army of the Potomac. O'Sullivan is credited with the famed "Harvest of Death" scene at Gettysburg. And there were such cameramen as Lewis H. Landy, T. C. Roche, James Gardner, D. B. Woodbury, J. Rookie and J. F. Coonley; these and others are obscure today, with little information available anywhere about their activities.

But Mathew B. Brady was no mere desk editor, a dispatcher who sat on a soft chair and sent others to combat. Whenever possible, he went where the action was, into some of the bloodiest battles—Bull Run, Antietam, Fredericksburg, Gettysburg, Petersburg, and the entire nine-month campaign to capture Richmond. He took as much risk as any photographer who films battle, showing no more nor less courage than his assistants. At Petersburg, he stood at the side of Union artillery to make photographs—and continued his shooting even when Confederate cannon shelled the Union battery. Shells fell around him, throwing up clumps and clouds of dirt, but he stood his ground—very close to death.

Danger, financial disaster, discouragement and disappointment—Brady stood them off throughout the Civil War, working with a compulsive eye to posterity. Once he had proved that war photography was practical —perhaps even profitable—competitors leaped in. The Anthonys, a rival firm, even pirated some of his crew, the first being Thomas C. Roche. In 1863 Alexander Gardner left to open his own camera corps, taking with him some of Brady's top photographers. Evidently they were disenchanted because they did not get by-line credit for their photographs. In the case of Gardner, Brady probably could not pay his talented friend. According to biographer James Horan, "This is borne out by the fact that Brady gave Gardner a duplicate set of his battlefield wet plates, possibly in lieu of past wages."

After the Civil War, Mathew Brady had a huge collection of photographs, stored in warehouses; his commercial operation had declined; his wife was ill; and he was broke. He tried to rebuild his business, but success now eluded him, even though many illustrious Americans still wanted to be photographed by Brady. The government stalled on buying his great Civil War gallery—stalled until it was too late and Brady had to give up his collection to pay old debts. The rhythm of his life, of success and fame and fortune, seemed to have been fractured by the grandness of his achievement. His life after the war, until his death in 1896, was an anticlimax, a kind of holding action against the gloom of decline. Debts and then bankruptcy. Then his wife died. Sadness and loneliness. Finally, the retreat into obscurity.

Toward the end he was a gentle, quiet man, perhaps embittered, maybe dreaming of the glorious faces and scenes he had filmed, of Lincoln and Lee and Grant, of the yellow cornfields of Antietam and the misty hills of Gettysburg.

True to his self, he wrote no final will, scribbled no parting words, dictated no message of great meaning for future generations. Yet he was not inscrutable. Despite the few confusing facts about his birth and birthplace, about his early years and marriage and background—facts history too often rates as significant—the meaning of his life was clear and simple. It is as clear and simple as the thousands of wet plates, portraits and scenes and battlefields, now safely stored in the National Archives.

He was a child of destiny, who became the father of war photography, and did first what nobody has ever done better. His photographs are a mosaic of a nation rent, of faces torn by passion and anxiety, of blood spilled to bind up a union. Somewhere, at some unspecified moment, in a rare philosophical utterance, Mathew B. Brady spoke his own epitaph: "The camera is the eye of history . . . you must never make bad pictures." He never did.

Photographer Jimmy Hare moving up.

Jimmy Hare

3. The Intrepid Jimmy Hare

IN FEBRUARY, 1898, a wiry little man bounded into the offices of *Collier's* weekly. Bristling with determination, he rushed into the den of editor Robert J. Collier and delivered his "pitch" on the run. *Collier's* must send him to Cuba. War would soon be declared, and the magazine *had* to have a talented cameraman on hand. It simply *had* to have photographs immediately of the *Maine*, blown up in the harbor of Havana. It *had* to have portraits of Spanish leaders, soldiers and statesmen, and of the hapless Cubans held in concentration camps. And the man to do the job was Jimmy Hare.

Pelted by the barrage of words—and perhaps captivated by the photographer's enthusiasms and salesmanship—editor Robert Collier gave in.

During the Balkan War this Bulgarian bombardier dropped this aerial bomb—one of the first ever dropped from the air—upon the Turks. (By Jimmy Hare)

Above: Hare crept up close to shoot this view of the Spanish-American War.
Below: Americans hunted house to house for guerrillas in Mexico.

Military observers from great nations studied battlefield in the Russo-Japanese War. Later they spotted Jimmy Hare zigzagging across the plain below.

Now that he thought about it, *Collier's* did have to have a correspondent in Cuba. And, yes, Jimmy Hare would do nicely and could leave tomorrow if he could make the proper arrangements. Describing the tableau later to his staff, Robert Collier captured the spirit of America's most incredible news photographer: "The *Maine* blew up, and Jimmy blew in," he said. "Both were major explosions."

The adventures and exploits of Jamés Henry Hare have an incredible ring to the contemporary ear and strain a reader's capacity for belief. But his photographs are indisputable proof that he was indeed a central character in some of the most improbable, dangerous—and one is tempted to say, *hare-brained*—episodes in the history of journalism. The Spanish-American War, the Russo-Japanese War, two disturbances in Mexico and one in Venezuela, the first Balkan War, World War I and the Polish struggle against Russia—Jimmy Hare survived these and innumerable antics involving runaway balloons, pioneer airplaning, fires, earthquakes, floods and strikes. He darted across numerous battlefields, ducking shrapnel and rifle bullets, and performed remarkable feats of stamina for a lightweight man. He was only five-feet-two-inches tall but he conquered everything in his path—except water, his deadliest enemy. If a stream or a river or an ocean were near, he somehow managed to fall in, much to the glee of fellow journalists, who watched Hare as closely as current events.

Yet Jimmy Hare was no clown; no photographer of his day could rival his craftsmanship or his uncanny ability to capture history in the making. In a day when journalists were as flamboyant as the news they covered, he was one of the big ones, a friend of Richard Harding Davis, Jack London, Floyd Gibbons, Heywood Broun and the brilliant American author Stephen Crane. These men, and many others, including generals, statesmen, princes and presidents, admired his skill and courage.

He was born in London, England, October 3, 1856. His father, George Hare, was one of the world's finest manufacturers of handmade cameras. Jimmy, an indifferent student, left school at age sixteen and became an apprentice in his dad's shop. There he got a thorough, on-the-job education in photography. Camera bodies were made from wood then, and he acquired a love of fine craftsmanship, and a high respect for precision instruments and how to assemble them. The latter would stand him in good stead when he had to take apart a camera in the field. When he first learned picture-making, wet plates were used. Dry plates became popular in the 1870s, followed by cut film and, later, paper roll film.

Jimmy embraced each change, but his father grumbled at innovation. A conflict loomed between the impatient, independent son and the old-fashioned, conservative father. Jimmy was spunky and adventuresome, and to head off a clash with his father he decided to take a job in London with another camera company. He was happy in his new job and soon got married and began to raise a family. And he began taking more and more photographs, selling his stuff to illustrated magazines and experimenting with the latest equipment, including the first Kodak cameras.

In 1889, E. and H. T. Anthony & Company of New York offered him a job as technical advisor in their camera plant. He went to America, remained with the Anthony Company for a year, and then resigned to open his own factory. Although he was fairly successful manufacturing quality cameras, he was destined for a more exciting life. He became a

full-time news photographer on the staff of the *Illustrated American*, remaining with the publication until a fire wiped it out in 1898. When the *Maine* blew up in Havana, it launched Jimmy Hare's fantastic career as a war photographer. He was forty-two years old when he set sail for Cuba, the first battleground he would challenge.

He had no official credentials as a war correspondent; he had skipped the formalities in his eagerness to get where the action was. He knew very little about combat, but he charged into battle with abandon, determined to get photographs. At Kettle Hill he didn't even have a jug of water, and when an American private offered him a drink, he drained the canteen. An officer promptly scolded him for taking water from a poor soldier who might not be able to replace it for hours. Jimmy Hare was so ashamed he grabbed the canteen, leaped out of the trench and raced downhill through a shower of shells to replenish the water. He got back safely, an incredible performance that astonished the troops.

In the course of the Cuban campaign, Jimmy had enough adventures to wear out the strongest soldier of fortune. The short but hectic war found him aground on an oceangoing tug, wading ashore in waist-high water, plodding through mosquito-infested jungle, riding a horse over treacherous trails and sailing a small boat into gunfire from an American warship. He suffered from hunger and fever, was lashed by wind and rain, was thrown from a horse into a river and was shot at countless times.

During the battle of San Juan Hill, Jimmy took as many chances as the troops charging up the slope. Watching the soldiers crawl forward through tall grass, he felt that rear-view shots wouldn't excite the readers of *Collier's*. The solution seemed simple: he would get ahead of the troops and photograph their faces as they advanced. He ran up the hill, turned, and began making pictures of soldiers of the Sixth Infantry as they crept along. Then he decided to go down to get a panoramic view. He walked quickly, as though taking a brisk morning stroll, head bowed, concentrating against the hail of shrapnel. Two hundred yards down he focused his camera on the action above, snapped the shutter and prepared to leave. Before he could move, a horse's head looked over his shoulder and gave him something of a start.

Mounted on a pinto and wearing a shiny white raincoat—a perfect target, of course!—was Stephen Crane, as nonchalant as though sitting behind a desk. Crane convinced Jimmy to go back up the hill, through fire again, and into one of the deadliest points, a spot later called "The Bloody Bend." Dozens and dozens of wounded huddled under an overhanging riverbank, receiving first aid under shellfire. Jimmy Hare and Stephen Crane survived this and other perilous situations in the battle, perhaps because their insouciance bewildered the enemy. Crane and Hare were exceptionally cool under fire, and in the eyes of some onlookers, downright foolish—*un poco loco*, as the Spanish say.

Stephen Crane, author of *The Red Badge of Courage*, had never seen war before, although his novel was as vivid and realistic as any book ever written on the subject. But he wanted to see how men acted in action, what danger really felt like, and was silly enough to court death, once standing in the open and drawing rifle fire, a performance that infuriated Colonel Leonard Wood of the Rough Riders. Before Cuba, Jimmy Hare had naive notions about battle—notions based on old-fashioned paintings of European armies parading shoulder to shoulder, and then lining up in ranks to fire at one another. Men crawling on their bellies or firing out of trenches was news to him. So the Spanish-American War made him a veteran in a hurry, preparing him for other bloody engagements.

For the next few years Jimmy Hare covered the news as it broke. His only brushes with war were two trips into the Southern Hemisphere, to Venezuela and Panama, when violence threatened. These engagements turned out tamely, episodes of bluster and shouting rather than serious shooting. But in 1903 deadly war storms were shaping up in Asia in a war that would send Jimmy Hare halfway around the world.

Russia and Japan were squaring off, and before blows were struck, *Collier's* wanted a team of reporters on the field. Among those scheduled to sail for the Orient were Jimmy Hare and Richard Harding Davis, whom Jimmy had befriended in Cuba. On the liner going over Jimmy met another famous author, Jack London, who was immediately impressed by the photographer's scrappy nature (Jimmy challenged a correspondent twice his size to a fistfight).

In February, 1904, the Japanese sank the Russian cruiser *Variag* and the gunboat *Korietz*. Japan was being inundated with foreign correspondents, all eager to get to the front. The war office decided to issue only fifteen permits, and Jimmy Hare got one. After much delay and stalling by Japanese authorities—who were masters of evasive action—Jimmy arrived in Korea. There he had to use all his charm and ingenuity to outwit Japanese censors. At that time correspondents were free-wheeling characters, unaccustomed to military censorship, which was in its infancy and would become a major headache for reporters trying to cover World War I. (Today, of course, censorship has been refined by governments who "manage" the news.)

Jimmy and other newsmen had to get to the battlefield on their own; governments did not provide transportation then as they do today. The correspondents organized a caravan, including personal coolies, camping equipment, food and horses. Their destination was the Yalu River, the boundary between Korea and Manchuria, where they expected a big battle. During the safari north, Jimmy's horse skidded off a small bridge and the photographer went into a stream, soaking himself and all his equipment. It was his second horse-and-water fiasco—the first came in Cuba—and he was forced to remain behind to dry his equipment. The next day, he set out after the main party, this time pedaling furiously along on a bicycle! It got him to the front well in advance of action.

When the Japanese and Russians began shelling each other at the Yalu, Jimmy Hare decided to slip away from the hilltop observation area reserved for correspondents. From there it was impossible to photograph the battle, and he was bored by the small view offered through binoculars.

Jimmy mounted his horse and, when officialdom was looking the other way, sneaked off toward the lines. Following him on foot was his Japanese servant, Kurataki, carrying a heavy panoramic camera. The two truants managed to mingle with the troops crossing the bridgehead to an island in the Yalu, which they had to ford. Thus he was in Manchuria while the rest of the press stood on a hill watching the scene through binoculars. Pushing on, he photographed men charging ahead, dropping to their stomachs and rising to advance again under a cover of support artillery. He returned to the river and made pictures of wounded returning from the battle and being treated in field tents. When he decided to return to base, he discovered that the closest pontoon bridge had been blown up by Russian cannon. He took a roundabout course to return to camp, and was at the big bridgehead on the Yalu when the rest of the correspondents, escorted by their Japanese hosts, started to cross. With a flourish, Jimmy Hare welcomed them all to Manchuria; they in turn praised his ingenuity, despite the fact that he had scooped the world.

Jimmy Hare was then a middle-aged man and without a doubt one of the sturdiest little correspondents ever to roam a battlefield. After taking his exclusive photographs, he had to develop the film in a tent and then dry the pictures. The weather was dreary and damp and the film had to be hung up and dried by waving lighted candles in front of it. In the biography *Jimmy Hare, News Photographer*, Cecil Carnes quoted a *Collier's* article praising the intrepid cameraman:

> I wonder if those who saw the realistic pictures of the groups of wounded around the hospital tents at the Yalu realized at all what they cost this little man, who is nearing his fiftieth year. He was the first of the correspondents' corps to cross the river. He trudged through miles of sand up to his knees. His pony was worn out; his weary servant promptly resigned. But Jimmy himself was up the next morning at daybreak, ill and pale, developing the first photographs of the army at the front to be published.

As the Japanese pushed into Manchuria, Jimmy blanketed their activities—bridge building, artillery fire, camouflaging, reserves rushing up, infantry charges, and wounded streaming into temporary hospitals. And he charmed the censors into passing his stuff by first showing them pictures of Japanese soldiers treating Russian prisoners with great kindness, offering water from their canteens and distributing cigarettes. In his efforts to get exclusive photographs he drew on great stamina, imagination and courage. When the Japanese laid siege to Liao-yang, the affair dragged on too long for the impatient photographer, so he decided to slip into the town ahead of the attackers. He had to take a roundabout course, and, in the process, got lost and wandered about for five days, with little to eat or drink. When he reached the town, only a few Japanese scouts were there, waiting for the main body of troops. When the

Japanese arrived in force, columns of infantry four-abreast, there stood James H. Hare to record their victorious entrance. Again he had scooped everybody, for most of the correspondents never got into Liao-yang.

Jimmy Hare was incapable of watching war from a distance, and his impatience with the long-range view compelled him to play a reckless role. Perhaps his most reckless performance took place one hot day in Manchuria as the Japanese drove toward Mukden. Foreign correspondents and military observers were standing on a hill watching artillery fire on a small village. Perhaps in jest, a Japanese challenged Jimmy to go down and photograph the shelling—and that was all Hare needed. Off he jogged, on a straight line into danger.

From the safety of the hill, observers followed his progress through field glasses, marveling at his colossal nerve. In the village, the brash photographer secured a ladder and climbed to the roof of a house, and then made several exposures as shells whistled overhead. Frightened villagers huddled in dugouts, staring in disbelief as Jimmy Hare descended the ladder and took off to join some Japanese troops in a trench several hundred yards away. There he waited a few minutes as Russian artillery shells exploded all around. Next he ran straight to a Japanese battery and began making pictures of concealed gun emplacements, much to the rage of the gunners, who feared he'd give their location away. So Jimmy galloped off again, this time in the most incredible dash in the annals of war photography.

He sprinted across the plain, dropping to the ground as shells burst yards from his heel or directly ahead. He noticed that the shells fell at regular intervals of about fifty yards apart, as though the Russians were elevating their fire in a regular pattern to spray the field. Off went the wild Hare again, trying to time his run to the line of fire, so that he would always be fifty yards away from a bursting shell! He gave up this insane sprint when he decided to photograph the puffs of smoke made by exploding shrapnel. To do this he had to kneel to one side of the line of fire and guess when and where the shell would burst. He succeeded in making the photograph. That he accomplished this and returned with a whole skin was considered a miracle by the observers on the hilltop.

Jimmy Hare spent eight months covering the Russo-Japanese War, returning to the states when winter drew on and the war became a waiting game. After the war, he received a medal from the Emperor of Japan. A diploma, a rather ornate document, accompanied it, stating that James Henry Hare had served on active duty as a correspondent to the Imperial Army. This presentation made it official: he had earned his Master's Degree as a war photographer.

For the next few years, he photographed the news and occasionally was its key character. In 1906, he made the first aerial view of Manhattan, soaring over the city in a balloon. In the spring of the same year, he covered the San Francisco earthquake and fire. When the Wright brothers conquered the air at Kitty Hawk, Jimmy Hare took the first picture of an airplane in flight. In 1909, he made the first photograph of a President and a President-Elect, Theodore Roosevelt and William Howard Taft, on Inauguration Day. In 1911, he took the first photographs ever made from an airplane. Also, in 1911, he covered the revolution in Mexico, in which Francisco I. Madero ousted General Porfirio Díaz. Again he demonstrated his courage and ingenuity, particularly during the fighting in Juarez, and he convinced the notorious bandit, Pancho Villa, who disliked Americans, to pose for pictures on the roof of a hotel. In 1912, Jimmy crossed the ocean to cover the Balkan War. When war threatened between the U. S. and Mexico in 1913, he headed south again, covering fighting in Vera Cruz, San Gregori and Xochimilco. He was in Mexico City in August, 1914, when England declared war on Germany; he immediately cabled *Collier's* for permission to go to Europe. When the magazine refused, Jimmy Hare, determined to go at all costs, left *Collier's* and signed a contract with *Leslie's Weekly*.

Off he sailed to war again, nearly fifty-eight years old but as enthusiastic and frisky as a cub reporter. World War I was frustrating for correspondents, and Jimmy spent a good deal of time cutting through red tape to get to the front. His travels in the next two years make today's commuter look like a homebody. By the spring of 1916, his trail read like this: New York . . . London . . . Paris . . . Villers-Cotterêts . . . . . . Paris . . . London . . . Antwerp . . . London . . . Calais . . . London

. . . Paris . . . London . . . the French front . . . Rome . . . Salonika

. . . Marseilles . . . Paris . . . the Vosges . . . Paris . . . New York. During his first trip to the front, at Villers-Cotterêts, he was stopped by an English colonel, who refused to permit photographs. But he managed to get some good shots of the shelling in Antwerp and of the Belgian Army blowing up the bridges to cover their retreat. In Greece, he took some fine pictures of the British and French fronts and was permitted to photograph the quays and camps of Salonika. But he was hounded constantly by censors and officers demanding his credentials, and decided to go home for a rest.

After a vacation, Jim Hare went back overseas and this time was permitted to cover action at the Somme. The front, Paris, London—a few more months of commuting and he was recalled by *Leslie's*, who anticipated America's entrance in the war. Back home, he covered the training of doughboys before he sailed for Italy in March, 1918. At Padua, he photographed King Victor Emmanuel reviewing troops—and enraged a colonel of military police who wanted to arrest him. At the Piave River, when the Italians threw back the Austrians in a major battle, a shell fell near Jimmy, but his famous luck held. The shell did not explode. Yet he continued to take daring chances, crawling toward the trenches despite sharp-shooting Austrians.

Jimmy got through World War I, and in 1920 made one more trip into trouble, visiting Russia. Then he traveled to Warsaw to cover the fighting between Poland and Russia. From there he crossed the Dnieper River, to the east of Kiev, and then back to Warsaw, heading home, tired of the sight of dying soldiers, of broken equipment and ravaged villages. It was his last safari to war.

James Henry Hare had a breathtaking career as a war photographer—the jungles and hills of Cuba, the plains of Manchuria, the streets of Mexico, the trenches of Europe. He challenged death time after time, pioneering modern war photography. He was the first great action photographer and set a record for longevity and stamina that may never be equaled. He was sixty-four when he decided to retire as a war correspondent. He died in 1946, shortly before his ninetieth birthday; his credo of daring—"you can't get good battle pictures without taking chances"—is *the* canon of war photography.

41

André Kertesz, soldier and candid cameraman in World War I.

André Kertesz

October 23, 1916: A Hungarian soldier at ease with music. (Photos by André Kertesz)

October, 1918: Troops prepare to leave Transylvania, Rumania. July, 1915 (below): Austro-Hungarian soldiers wind their way toward the front.

In this candid photo, taken in 1915, a young soldier writes a letter home.

4. The Joy of Discovery

THE ABILITY to see and feel, to distinguish one object from another by sight and to respond to pain and pleasure, belongs to all normal babies at birth. But the blessing of pure vision and fresh feeling, of selecting and organizing experience with originality, is a gift rarely bestowed on an adult. It is the essence of art—of painting, of music, of poetry. Where does this uniqueness come from? How does it develop? What actually is it?

Most painters and poets and composers can be analyzed, their backgrounds studied, their growth charted until a general picture of their creative wellsprings emerges. Yet there are a few who seem to spring upon the scene fully developed, with points of view mysteriously acquired from a source heaven only knows. They are truly unique, for they do not seem to plan their creative acts; they simply act—compose, paint, make photographs. André Kertesz is such a man; his entire life has been a voyage of pure vision, following the path of self-discovery.

A born photographer, he is the inventor of what we call "candid photography," and of modern photo reportage. He was taking candid reportorial pictures before the development of the first fine miniature camera, the Leica, with which so many superb photographers would make reputations. Before Dr. Erich Salomon or Alfred Eisenstaedt appeared on the scene, Kertesz had perfected his technique. His great work pointed the way for such brilliant photographers as Henri Cartier-Bresson and Gyula Brassaï—and he started before World War I.

Born July 2, 1894, in Budapest, André Kertesz was the second of three surviving sons of Leopold and Ernestine Kertesz. His father was a bookseller, and young André's life was warm and pleasant, with no undue hardships. He was a poetic youngster. Carefree about school, he loved to play hookey. When he was twelve he ran away from home out of pure joy and gypsyism, taking with him a flute, a book and a few pennies in his pocket.

His city companions were students of art, and he acquired from them the values of the artist, a sense of integrity, honesty, a spirit of independence, a carefree attitude and zest for experience.

His father died when the boy was fifteen, and André was raised by an uncle, a stockbroker. He graduated from the Academy of Commerce in 1912, and took a job as a bookkeeper, largely to please his family, who had middle-class notions about a suitable career for the youngster. But as soon as André could save enough money he bought a camera and began making photographs. From the beginning his pictures were brilliantly original, showing a sure hand and a clarity of purpose. He was eighteen years old; he knew that he must express himself through photography—and, most remarkable, expressed himself sensitively with a primitive box camera that used glass plates. One of his first photographs, showing a boy sleeping with his hand cupped to one ear, is a miniature moment of truth.

There is eagerness and love of people in the early pictures of Kertesz, who saw life with an innocent eye. Untrained and untutored, with no formal background in painting or photography, he focused directly on what he saw, trying to express what he felt. It was pure intuition, as natural to him as breathing, of looking at a scene or situation and recording it as though with a glance. The glance was deeply human. He loved experience and was captivated by the freshness of new people and places.

He was drafted into the Hungarian Army in 1914 and served in Central Europe, in Austria, Albania, Rumania and Galicia. In Poland, in 1915, he was shot over the heart and suffered a complete paralysis of his left hand for a year. An experimental operation was performed, and to convalesce he was sent to take charge of a small Russian prison camp on the Black Sea. In addition to this serious wound, Kertesz was hospitalized with typhoid fever. When he returned to the field, he learned that his entire regiment had been captured.

During the war, André Kertesz became a pioneer of a new style of war photography—the candid—although he was unaware of it at the time. He was a soldier, taking pictures in spare moments, in the trenches and when the troops moved up to the front. Since he was not making pictures in any official capacity, the making of them was a special labor of love. He carried a small camera and heavy little glass plates in his knapsack and made snapshots of soldiers and civilians caught up in war. Again, he simply was doing what came naturally to him, capturing on film little slices of life. "Expressing myself—that has always been the thing with me," he said recently. "A photographer should put human feeling on film. Not make a catalogue."

War horrified him, as it does any sensitive person. The sadness of seeing children and women uprooted, of walking into an empty house, still warm from a dying fire, but without people to be cheered by its flames—the memory moves him to this day. Yet he does not believe that war was a major factor in the development of his work. For him there has not been any single event which has contributed to personal growth —for the simple reason that he does not see his life as a series of events. "I never analyze," he once told the author. "I just express."

His war photographs—and only a few were not lost in the Revolution of 1918—are like a little diary, personally kept by a single soldier, perhaps to show to his folks or to old comrades back home after the cannons were stilled. But it is really doubtful if he did have any sense of purpose in taking them—taking them merely because the act itself was part of his existence. Most of the pictures show individuals caught by circumstances beyond their control and comprehension: soldiers and civilians swept by a tide of violence. Troops moving up, a soldier parting from his wife, a man sifting rubble for a cigarette butt, cavalrymen preparing to mount up—these are the tableaus of war as he saw it.

He shows a company of Polish troops standing with heads bowed, observing Mass before a battle. Or, in a little gem of a picture, there is a bearded warrior waiting to embark from Brailia, Rumania. He is sitting on a cobbled street, a rifle cradled in his arms, his back against a supply wagon. In the foreground, almost (but not quite) like a separate photograph, are two small dogs sitting peacefully—an incongruous complement to the stacked rifles nearby. There is a very touching photograph of a youthful soldier sitting at a table in a barracks, writing a letter. His face is softly molded by the light, and in the background is another soldier, out of focus, glancing sideways, perhaps at the photographer.

These were the kind of war photos pioneered by Kertesz, and it is sad that so many were lost, because they were so fresh, and as human as a family album—a family album put together, with affection, by a genius. Kertesz's war photos, casual though they seem, were the forerunners of all the fine candid pictures taken in the 1930s (particularly in the Spanish Civil War), during World War II, the Korean struggle and on into the battles of the 1960s. And he took them with a clumsy little camera, without the benefit of high-speed film or superb interchangeable lenses.

The photographs of André Kertesz appear so simple that they could disarm us, except for one significant element—the element of the unexpected that shimmers with the light of revelation. A blind beggar playing a fiddle, his son at his side, stops in midstride, bow suspended above strings, "staring" at the camera. In the background, just a shade blurry, an infant stands trapped by time . . . A mustachioed man in a café, holding a glass of wine and glaring at the photographer (maybe at life), his wooden peg leg poised in counterpoint . . . A full-face portrait of Piet Mondrian, a direct and commonplace image—except that the painter's moustache, like his paintings, is off center! . . . These photographs could only have been taken by a man who moves from experience to experience, searching with joyous eye for miniature discoveries.

After World War I, Kertesz returned to Hungary and dutifully picked up his former life in the world of business, occasionally publishing pictures in Hungarian magazines. He simply was marking time until his family could be reconciled to his true calling. In 1925, he recalled many years later, his mother told him, "André, you are perfectly right to want to go away. There is nothing here for you."

He went to Paris, beginning his serious career, working to establish himself, mingling with the artistic colony of that capital of artists. Those were the days when picture magazines were starting, first in Germany and then in France. Kertesz worked as a free-lancer for the great publication *Vu*, and for *Art et Médecine*, *Variétés*, and *Bifur*. He was respected, a pacesetter and precursor, admired by young photographers. He became successful—although, he said years later, "I never made much money." French critics compared his work to that of Utrillo, Holbein, Hokusai and Courbet. His realism, his poetic eye, bittersweet and witty, his sense of irony and incongruity—his photographs captivated observers.

In 1936, Kertesz moved to the United States, where he has lived ever since, becoming a citizen in 1944. Although he worked for years for Condé Nast publications—*Vogue, Harper's Bazaar, Town and Country, House and Garden*—his career here has not been artistically rewarding. The framework of American magazines was much too rigid to tolerate a "natural" such as Kertesz. His pictures were too unexpected, not documentary in the standard sense, too individualistic—they "talked too much," as one *Life* editor told him. So for years this remarkable maker of unpredictable images suffered an undeserved obscurity in a nation flooded with mediocre graphics. However, lately there have been signs that his work has not been completely buried in the past.

In 1964, the Museum of Modern Art gave him a one-man exhibition; and in 1963, the American Society of Photographers and Journalists made him a member of honor, with this commendation:

"To André Kertesz, one of the greatest pioneers of photography, whom all photojournalists owe a great deal for his work and who for more than fifty years has been watching everyday life, discovering it in his simple and sensitive pictures."

André Kertesz continues to take pictures, looking through a viewfinder with kindly, incredibly alert eyes, searching constantly for some bright diamond in the human scene. He continues because he is blessed with purity of vision, and because seeing is his renewal. "I still feel young," he said in 1966. No doubt he always will.

SECTION II
A MODERN QUINTET

Margaret Bourke-White, the most glamorous war photographer.

Margaret Bourke-White

1. The Compleat Bourke-White

THE SHIPS bucked and fishtailed like a string of angry broncos. Boiling waves shot fifty feet high, turning the sea into canyons and cliffs of water. The big aircraft carrier tilted wildly and threatened to capsize. Sailors on tiny corvettes lashed themselves to the decks to keep from flying into the ocean. After five days in the violent Atlantic, the nurses and soldiers aboard the troopship were green and weak from seasickness, and so they smiled with relief when the convoy steamed by Gibraltar into the placid Mediterranean. Now, they could look to smooth sailing—so they thought.

The torpedo struck at midnight, and a photographer joined the flood

Korea, 1952: A mother welcomes her son home from war. (Life *photos by Margaret Bourke-White*)

of men and women heading for the deck. She stationed herself high above the flow of people, hoping for a picture in the moonlight. When the order came to abandon ship, Margaret Bourke-White felt her mouth go dry with fear.

"In a way I find hard to put into words," she wrote years later in *Portrait of Myself*, "the few minutes while we waited to step from the doomed ship into the flooded lifeboat have become for me almost a religious experience. I look back on it as a dividing time in my life—not in the sense of 'If I live it will be on borrowed time'; this was something that went much deeper with me and forged closer links with my fellow man. We stood—all six thousand of us—at a crossroads, not just between personal death or life but between paralyzing self-concern and that thought for others that transcends self. We were in a situation too vast for any one person to control, a catastrophe where people will show the qualities they have."

Danger, violence, action—they are not aliens in the world of Margaret Bourke-White, one of the most remarkable women of the twentieth century. She gives no ground to adversity, or to the flutter of fear; she faces them squarely. Embracing fresh experiences, she extracts gold from each to give new luster to her being. Of course, when writing of her, there is a lurking temptation to scatter adjectives with lavish hand. Her accomplishments are so sweeping, her life so full; she has created her own pedestal by refusing to stand above the turmoil of her time. She has developed her gifts with superbness, visually and verbally functioning on a superior level. A brilliant photographer, author of six books and co-author of four others, lecturer and radio commentator, she is a "compleat" commentator. That she also is beautiful and gallant makes her seem a demi-goddess. But though her achievements and attributes are formidable, there still is a stark simplicity and matter-of-factness about her. She is levelheaded.

War can rattle the calmest, but "Maggie," or Peggy, as she's sometimes called managed to cope with its hardships with the coolness of a trooper. When the S. S. *Strath-Allan* sank off North Africa, she was among those rescued by American destroyers and taken to Algiers. There, after a short rest, she went back into action aboard a B-17 on a bombing run over Tunis. Decked out in fleece-lined flying togs, the first American woman to become an accredited war correspondent, she brought a touch of glamour to the grim profession. Beginning in 1941, when she covered the German invasion of Russia, through World War II and the Korean war, she has photographed more combat than any other woman—and more than most men.

Her early years, her environment and interests, the development of her mind, character and personality—all these made adventure and achievement inevitable.

Her father, Joseph White, was an engineer and inventor; imaginative and ingenious, he was fascinated by machinery, by how it worked and how its uses could be expanded. He worked on ways to develop offset

Taken at the Buchenwald concentration camp, this great photograph is an everlasting indictment of Nazi Germany and the horrors it conceived.

lithography. During Margaret White's early years, she recalls that their home was a virtual laboratory as her father sought to perfect four-color printing: calendars, magazine covers, prints in various stages of separation—reds, yellows, blues. Joseph White took his daughter to factories and foundries, and these visits aroused in her the urge to capture the beauty of machines in motion.

From her father, she also acquired a passion for nature and dreamed of becoming a famous herpetologist. Growing up in Bound Brook, New Jersey, she took nature hikes in the nearby Watchung Mountains and kept a menagerie of turtles and other reptiles. One of her clearest recollections is the sight of her mother reading in front of a fireplace—a harmless puff adder curled in her lap.

Her father taught her to "never leave a job until you have done it to suit yourself and better than anyone else requires you to do it." Her mother, Minnie Bourke, had a broad, inquiring mind and was almost Prussian in her strictness: she forbade her son and two daughters to read the funny papers or visit homes where they were read. She was firm but certainly no tyrant; Margaret recalls her with love and admiration. For she was a person to be reckoned with—a person with a passion for honesty and truth, qualities which are the backbone of artistry. She discouraged the easy path; hard work and intellectual discipline were essential to sound character and success. Writing in her autobiography, *Portrait of Myself*, Bourke-White recalled:

> If my sister or I took one of the school examinations where you were required to answer only ten questions out of twelve, mother's comment on hearing this would be: "I hope you chose the ten hardest ones."

An apprehensive child, Peggy learned self-control—what Hemingway called "grace under pressure"—from her mother. "Go right up and look fear in the face—and then do something," her mother advised. This was the best advice an adventuresome girl could get. She was destined to participate in turbulent events: in the U. S., through the Depression and Dust Bowl era, and the building of great dams and power plants; in the U. S. S. R., through its first five-year plan; in India, during the chaos of shaping a free nation; around the world, in reconstruction and revolu-

Russia, 1941: Night bombing of the Kremlin as captured by Margaret Bourke-White.

tion—and in war. When she set off for college, she embarked on a career that would take her into thirty-six countries—and may yet take her into space, if she gets her wish to photograph the moon for *Life* magazine.

"Adventure must start with running away from home," wrote William Bolitho in *Twelve Against the Gods.* Bolitho's brilliant insight should be broadened: adventure starts with leaving home, on the run or otherwise. It requires deserting the coziness of the living room for the chill of unknown, distant places. Danger and uncertainty are your companions; courage and resourcefulness your allies.

By the time she was twenty-one, Margaret had gone to seven colleges, had been married and divorced, had changed her name to Bourke-White, and had begun a photographic apprenticeship in Cleveland, Ohio. (Her father had died while she was in college, and, hard-pressed for cash, she began taking pictures at Cornell, where she received her bachelor's degree, majoring in biology.) Hard work, loneliness, poor pay—a struggling careerist must learn to endure, and for every moment of discouragement there is the joy of accomplishment.

Cleveland was perfect for the lovely, long-legged brunette; she fell in love with the steel mills and took the pictures that opened the door to recognition. There, in a short but intense two years, she learned the fundamentals of developing, printing, enlarging and "dodging." She also learned an important lesson from a photographic journeyman, Alfred Hall Bemis: "Don't worry about what the other fellow is doing. Shoot off your own guns." Her fiery determination was fusing a point of view; the shape was architectural, the beauty of pure lines, which framed a passion for the truth. It is this hard-core honesty that has enabled her to escape the fate of many talented photographers. For photography, like mathematics, tends to be a young man's—or young woman's—game and too many talents are stunted by success. The Steichens, the Westons and the Dorothea Langes are rare. Bourke-White belongs with the distinguished exceptions; she has the will to move on when a given experience has been exhausted.

After Cleveland came a call to New York, where a new magazine, *Fortune*, was about to open up American business and industry to pictorialization. Henry Luce, founder of *Time* and later of *Life*, saw immense significance and excitement in this day-to-day drama. Bourke-White's steel shots had caught his eye. And for her, this was the opportunity to fulfill the early dream of capturing the beauty of machines. Shoemaking, watchmaking, glassmaking—automobiles, toys, fishing equipment, factories and foundries—bridges and coal rigs, farming and logging—she crisscrossed America's workaday life. Then, in 1931, *Fortune* sent her to Russia to photograph the infant industrialization of the Soviets, and from this assignment came her first book, *Eyes on Russia*. Back in the United States, she continued her documentation of industry until, in 1934, she had a profound experience, which added another dimension to her vision. From deep in Texas to the far north of the Dakotas, wind and erosion had shaped a "dust bowl"—a living nightmare to those who lived close to the American earth.

"I think this was the beginning," she wrote, "of my awareness of people in a human, sympathetic sense as objects for the camera and photographed against a wider canvas than I had perceived before. During the rapturous period when I was discovering the beauty of industrial shapes, people were only incidental to me, and in retrospect I believe I had not much feeling for them in my earlier work. But suddenly it was the people who counted. Here in the Dakotas with these farmers, I saw everything in a new light. How could I tell it all in pictures? Here were the faces engraved with the very paralysis of despair. These were faces I could not pass by."

Her eyes opened to a new America, to the people of the earth who toiled and suffered greatly and were weighed down with despair. She began to think in terms of a book, but felt the project needed a powerful, polished writer. By great chance, it happened such a writer was not only available; he was considering a similar project—and searching for a photographer as collaborator. His name was Erskine Caldwell, author of *Tobacco Road* and other perceptive books about the South.

Beginning in 1936, they worked together for six years, collaborating on three books, the first of which, *You Have Seen Their Faces*, was a portrayal of the plight of the Southern sharecroppers. They traveled by car through Alabama, Georgia, Louisiana, the Carolinas—the South—exploring hot, dusty back roads where Caldwell chatted over back fences and on front porches with the citizens of poverty. When she wasn't taking pictures, Bourke-White listened to the conversations and learned how a fine writer won the trust of people by talking their language without patronization. Later she would see how Erskine Caldwell caught, with great subtlety, the character of the sharecropper through the intonations of speech. The photographer acquired a new depth of compassion and maturity that would mark her works to come.

"Many times in the sharecropper country," she recalled, "my thoughts went back to the Dakotas, where the farmers were stricken with the drought. Their very desperation had jolted me into the realization that a man is more than a figure to put into the background of a photograph for scale . . . here with the sharecroppers I was learning that to understand another human being you must gain some insight into the conditions which made him what he is. The people and the forces which shape them: each holds the key to the other. These are the relationships that can be studied and photographed."

The year 1936 was significant in her career: the first issue of *Life* (November 23) carried her photograph of Fort Peck Dam in Montana. For her, *Life* was exciting, *Life* was dramatic, fresh and zestful. Each assignment, every deadline, was merely a challenge to conquer the un-

59

expected. The racing events, the chaos of split-second preparation, the urgency of editorial demands—all were fodder to exhilarate her. The second inaugural of President Roosevelt, the terrible Louisville flood, the story of Mayor Hague in Jersey City, an adventurous trip to the Arctic—she winged from event to event, a breathtaking pace. A superb craftsman, poised, mature in thinking, she could not be thrown off balance. She always seemed to be where the action was, and in the next few years the arena would be war.

In 1939, she married Erskine Caldwell and they started on a trip which carried them nearly all the way around the world, turning up in Moscow a month before the Germans attacked Russia. When the blitzkrieg hit the U. S. S. R. in June, 1941, the American ambassador urged them to leave the capital for Vladivostok, in the east. The Caldwells insisted on staying. After all, Margaret was the only foreign photographer in the country at that time; she had a marvelous chance to scoop the world.

The early weeks of war found a frustrated photographer banging on the doors of bureaucracy, trying to get permission to use her cameras. Security and censorship, the twin enemies of correspondents, had her in handcuffs. But Bourke-White, a very persistent lady, pounded away at them until they wrote her a special pass to take pictures.

The Luftwaffe came over in waves, and the flares and tracers and incendiaries festooned the sky with deadly lights. The air attacks drove the Muscovites underground, but not the intrepid photographer. She photographed the bombings from the roof of the American embassy and from a hotel balcony. To do this at the hotel, she had to hide under the bed to escape the nightly search of air raid wardens whose job it was to shoo everyone into shelters. Once they had made their rounds, she could shoot the spectacle with single-minded concentration.

Once at the embassy she came very close to becoming a casualty. The bomb fell through the night with neither sound nor light to warn her but only that eerie contraction of air one senses when explosion is imminent. She scrambled through the window and flattened herself on the floor just before the windows of the embassy blew in, raining glass upon her. A big window ventilator sailed across the room, and had she been in its path a brilliant career would have been extinguished.

Life kept demanding pictures and she had to produce at a grueling pace. By day, she put on film the destruction in the city streets and atop the buildings, where women painted camouflage windows; the first enemy plane shot down; the first Nazi pilot captured; she went inside the Kremlin to photograph Josef Stalin. And every night at ten o'clock she was outside with her cameras aimed at the heavens. In between picture-making, she had to take notes, write captions, develop film, write letters and just plain endure. Their hotel suite looked like a command post for journalists: films in the bathtub developing, prints hanging to dry, manuscripts being typed and dispatched. Erskine Caldwell was writing at a furious pace to keep up with the offers for his services pouring in from publications around the world. And there were regular radio broadcasts—the first "live" shows by a foreigner—beamed from Moscow at 2 A. M., with the Caldwells alternating at the microphone.

In the fall of 1941, when the Germans swept across the Soviet Union, the Caldwells drove to the front near Smolensk. The road was a river of mud; trucks and cars slopped along, throwing up a curtain of chocolate which speckled the windshields. Occasionally, a vehicle mired itself fender-deep in the ooze, and stones and logs had to be laid beneath the wheels. An hour of this work and the men looked like muddy bears from head to toe. When the Luftwaffe dived from the bleak skies to attack the convoy, all hands stampeded from the vehicles and flung themselves facedown in the muddy meadows.

It was dangerous and depressing work for a photographer (and certainly no place for a lady). During a week at the front, Margaret Bourke-White estimated that she had sixteen minutes of sunlight. Then there was the horror and heartbreak of a land being destroyed by its own people in the so-called scorched-earth policy—dams blown up, crops burned, villages razed. German cannon and bombs reduced little farms and towns to rubble, killing civilians in the process. Once Bourke-White walked into a small courtyard and photographed a family of four lying dead in a doorway.

"It is a peculiar thing about pictures of this sort," she wrote in her book, *Shooting the Russian War*. "It is as though a protecting screen draws itself across my mind and makes it possible to consider focus and light values and technique of photography, in as impersonal a way as though I were making an abstract camera composition. This blind lasts as long as it is needed—while I am actually operating the camera. Days

61

later, when I developed the negatives, I was surprised to find that I could not bring myself to look at the films. I had to have someone else handle and sort them for me."

The Caldwells left Russia late in 1941 on a cargo ship, out of Archangel into the Arctic Ocean and the North Sea to Scotland, then flying on to Portugal and home. During the sea voyage, Bourke-White got a preview of war at sea as her convoy played peek-a-boo with Nazi subs. She slept on deck for two nights, wearing a steel helmet all the time and keeping her cameras at the ready. Fortunately, a fog enabled the lumbering ships to elude the sub pack.

After lecturing in the States and writing her book on Russia, Margaret Bourke-White was accredited to the U. S. A. F. and went to England, then to North Africa. In 1943, at the request of General Brehon Somervell, she went to Italy to cover the work of the Army Service of Supply, to give pictorial tribute to the men who slaved at an unglamorous but vital job. The superiority of American logistics would turn the tide of World War II and Bourke-White, with her flair for dramatizing machines and people, was the ideal photographer to document this aspect of the struggle.

Her arrival in Naples was timely, for the mighty task of clearing the harbor of scuttled ships was beginning. After recording this feat, she jeeped into one of the grimmest, most grinding battles of World War II. The Allies were trying to break through the mountains surrounding the Cassino Valley. The retreating Germans had blown up bridges over the wild mountain streams, and American engineers, using the famed "Bailey Bridge," were putting up new structures. The enemy, entrenched in the hills, had the valley zeroed in with heavy artillery and our troops were looking into the mouths of cannons.

Bourke-White covered the campaign on the ground and in the air. She photographed U. S. artillery firing their "long toms" (155 mm guns) at the enemy fortifications. One night she "drafted" soldiers as camera handlers, and by the end of the bombardment a Brigadier General was shooting pictures as she gave the command to fire!

In those days, helicopters hadn't been perfected, so small airplanes were used to spot enemy positions. She flew in a Piper Cub—a Grasshopper—to get aerial views, an extremely dangerous practice. Once, on a flight to spot a "screaming meemie" (a German howitzer), the little plane was pursued by four enemy fighters. The American pilot took extreme evasive action: he dived sharply *below* treetop level and zig-zagged along a stream bed to his home base.

During her five months in Italy, Bourke-White was under fire a lot—from bombs and artillery and machine guns—but managed to escape without a wound. She had her share of good luck and some bad luck, too. The bad luck—the kind a photographer fears worse than bullets—occurred when a package of film exposed under hazardous conditions, was lost somewhere in that government-built chaos, the Pentagon, Washington, D. C. The film was her tribute to the Medical Corps in action: gallant nurses and surgeons working under attack, truck drivers donating blood during bombardment, and the death of a brave soldier. (She would lose another package of film on her second mission to Italy, to photograph the "forgotten front," in 1944.) To counteract the bad luck, of course, there was the book she wrote about the bloody struggle: *They Called It Purple Heart Valley* turned out to be the most popular book she has done to date.

Her next book, *Dear Fatherland, Rest Quietly* (the title from *Watch on the Rhine*), came from a trip to Germany in 1945 to photograph the end of the Third Reich and the immediate aftermath. Published in 1946, it was one of the first books to attempt to penetrate the riddle of the German character and answer some puzzling questions. Who are the German villains? What do their faces look like? Why did they follow blindly the mad Fuehrer?

The answers were elusive, because the people chose to evade their responsibilities as citizens of humanity. As she went from place to place, photographing the victims of concentration camps and questioning the Germans—from Krupp to commoner—she heard the same refrain thousands of times: "We didn't know, we didn't know." It was an unbelievable Teutonic wail, sickening in self-pity, disgusting in self-deceit. At Buchenwald in April, 1945, she took a powerful photograph of prisoners whose eyes are glazed with a horror beyond human comprehension. This shows what can happen when human ingenuity is distorted to the ultimate degree of savagery. The Buchenwald photograph is one of the greatest commentaries on war ever made, and the photographer had to shoot it from behind a "protective veil" drawn tight to protect her from unbearable pain.

63

To escape the death and rot of Europe, Bourke-White went to India, a nation in the birth pangs of freedom. There she was privileged to observe the drama of a struggling nation and of its gentle leader, Mahatma Gandhi. She studied the man, the people, the environment for two years, and in 1949 published her report, *Halfway to Freedom*. It is first-rate, sober and compassionate and deep, perhaps her best book thus far. It is Bourke-White at her fullest, serene and sure, in command of material and métier. It illuminates her life style: the photos are taken, the experiences are lived—then comes the assimilation, the book.

She was not finished with war, though; her passion for people compelled her to go to Korea in 1952. "What were the Korean people doing?" she asked herself. "What were they saying and thinking?"

To get the answers, she went straight to the heart of danger, deep into Korea, into the back country where guerrillas hid in ambush. Carried by helicopters to remote areas, she would vanish for weeks at a time, sleeping on the ground or in such strange places as country police stations, miles away from safety and comfort.

Since she insisted on venturing farther and farther from secure areas—and since the Communists had put a price on her head as a dangerous photographer—the military grew more worried for her life. They finally insisted she carry a .45 pistol and a carbine, even though correspondents were forbidden to do so. When she protested that she had never fired a gun, they took her to the range. Her first day with the pistol she fired thirty-five rounds, scoring thirty-three bulls-eyes! Her first try with a carbine she fired twenty-five rounds. The result: twenty-five bulls-eyes. The instructor shook his head in astonishment: "My sympathy is all with the guerrillas," he said.

The heart of her photo essay on Korea was a single human family, one that would illustrate the divisiveness of war, of brother against brother and of ideas in opposition. One day she found her subject, a young man named Nim Churl-Jin. He had lived in a village in the south, had run away to fight with the Communists, and had been captured by South Koreans. He was disillusioned by the North Koreans and longed to return to his village and his mother, but feared the wrath of his older brother, a severe anti-Communist. Bourke-White followed him back to his home, and her photograph of the mother-son reunion is a universal comment on war and the family. It is symbolic of her point of view. Nothing is forced or faked, no tricks or gimmicks, no deliberate blurring or soft focusing. The truth is in the drama itself, in the subjects caught at a poignant moment and framed with architectural clarity.

Korea was her last experience with war, to date. She went there, she wrote in a letter, "because I felt that one side of the conflict wasn't covered and that was the story of the people themselves. I was convinced that the people couldn't be living in a vacuum. It seemed very important to me to find out what was going on and in doing so I ran into one of the most human stories it has ever been my chance to photograph."

Her mother had taught her to face fear squarely and then "do something" about it. She had called upon this talisman many times during war, and had to lean on it and all her resources when struck by a major illness in the 1950s. It began slowly with a pain in her left leg, followed by a slight lurch when she rose to walk.

The mysterious disease was finally diagnosed by Doctor Howard Rusk, world renowned for his work in the physical rehabilitation of polio victims. Margaret Bourke-White had Parkinson's Disease, which is considered incurable. It attacks that part of the brain which controls body movements; its symptoms are muscular weakness, a trembling of the hands and a rigidity of the limbs. America's great playwright Eugene O'Neill had it, and, because he wrote in longhand, had had to give up his career. Justice Harold H. Burton retired from the Supreme Court because of it. The disease can be controlled by dedicated, daily exercise —by squeezing a rubber ball to strengthen the hands, by walking four or five miles per day to build up leg muscles. But this regimen requires superb willpower and steely determination; it requires a Bourke-White.

Her gallant fight—rigorous exercising and two major operations—has been going on for more than a dozen years, and has been dramatized on television and written about in magazines and books. It is inspirational but not sentimental, because the fight is inevitable, given the indomitable character of Bourke-White. Writing a few lines a day, a few paragraphs a week over a ten-year period, she published *Portrait of Myself* in 1963. Surely there will be another book to come, for she is a "compleat" person, the kind who must produce as long as she lives.

Edward Steichen, in action on a carrier in World War II.

Edward Steichen

In his garden blooms a shad-blow tree.
Guarding the bank of a pond
Whose waters offer an arboreal mirror.
Flowering white in spring,
Red with berries in summer,
Golden-leafed in autumn,
A sentinel stark in winter white.
From shrub to shimmering elegance,
A mute subject for the artist's eye:
Recording with camera years of moods and changes.

2. The Long Apprenticeship

A MANTLE OF white hair, a magnificent, snowy beard—Edward Steichen stands tall and erect. Time has eroded his face, revealing flashes of his essence. His blue eyes are bright; sometimes impish and mocking, or intensely serious and sad, they reflect a long productive life. He is eighty-seven years old; his infatuation with photography goes back to the 1890s and has deepened, with changes of focus, into the 1960s. The career of Steichen has been kaleidoscopic, symbolic of nearly a century of dramatic development, in both the style and the substance of art and society. He has earned his reverential face through dedication to métier and through commitment to humanity. Superb craftsman, photo editor and museum director—he has given as much to photography as he has gained from it, and done more than any man alive to elevate the profession to a place among the fine arts.

Born in Luxembourg on March 27, 1879, Edward Jean Steichen was the only son of peasant parents, Jean Pierre and Marie (Kemp) Steichen. When Edward was eighteen months old the Steichens immigrated to Michigan, where his mother established a millinery shop and his father worked in the copper mines. In 1888, Edward was sent to the Pio Nono College near Milwaukee, Wisconsin, where the family settled the following year. At the age of fifteen, he left school to start a four-year apprenticeship as a designer in a local lithographic company. He started taking photographs in 1895 with a small, secondhand box camera, bought with money given him by his mother. (His mother, he wrote in his autobiograhy, *A Life in Photography*, was "The guiding and inspiring influence in my life, she was always an encouraging and a positive force.

This superb infrared photograph was taken on the U.S.S. Lexington. Sailors are preparing for the big strike on Kwajalein in 1943.

From my early childhood, she sought to imbue me with her own great strength and fortitude, her deep, warm optimism and human understanding.")

Steichen's first camera was the old-fashioned Kodak, the type of which its makers boasted: "You press the button, we do the rest." The sixteen-year-old novice bought a single roll of film, and his first exposure was of the family cat sleeping in the window of his mother's shop. Of the fifty roll exposures he took, only one was sharp and clear—a picture of his sister at the piano. His father thought that one successful photograph out of fifty was a poor average, but his mother said the one beautiful success compensated for forty-nine failures.

Shortly after, Steichen convinced his employer at the American Fine Art Company that the company ought to use photographs rather than old woodcuts for posters and showcards. They gave him time off to take pictures of pigs for a client, a pork-packing firm.

Trading his Kodak for a 4 x 5 view camera, which used plates instead of film, he soon had a darkroom set up in the family cellar and learned to develop and print. His pictures of pigs were much admired by the pork packers. This had an impact on him, for he recalled years later: "So my first real effort in photography was to make photographs that were useful. And, as I look back over the many intervening years, I find that usefulness has always been attractive in the art of photography."

Although he started out for a commercial purpose, a stronger, more personal image soon took over—the urge of the artist for self-expression. He began taking portraits of his friends and making landscapes and moody views of dusk and twilight; and he also painted in his spare time. He met with some fellows his own age and they rented an office, hired a model and made sketches of her. The group was called the Milwaukee Art Students' League, and Steichen was its first president. The members liked to discuss picture-making and debated the subject of sharp, clear photographs versus moody, "artistic" shots.

At that time, in 1897, Steichen was making haunting photographs of nature, of the woods and parks and fields outside Milwaukee. Although he wasn't aware of it, he was experimenting in "impressionism"—a poetic school of painting based on the concept of things and scenes as they appear at a given moment, rather than in permanent color and shape. His first recognition came in 1899, with "The Lady in the Doorway," an out-of-focus photograph exhibited at the Second Philadelphia Salon.

At age twenty-one, he quit his job at the lithographic company and set out for Paris to study painting. He stopped in New York City and met Alfred Stieglitz, the great photographer who was leading the battle to get photography recognized as art. Stieglitz encouraged the young cameraman, buying three of his prints for five dollars each. Steichen wrote about the meeting in his autobiography, recalling the parting scene.

As I left, he went with me to the elevator, and as the door closed, he said, "Well, I suppose now that you're going to Paris, you'll forget about photography and devote yourself entirely to painting."

As the elevator went down, I shouted up to him, "I will always stick to photography!"

The young Midwesterner found his first week in Paris "overwhelming," a bombardment of fresh experiences which struck him as being a form of "revelation," he later wrote. The sculpture of Rodin, the old masters at the Louvre, the Luxembourg, of living artists with one room given to the Impressionists—Monet, Degas, Pissarro and Sisley, whose shimmering handling of color and sunlight were entrancing—all stimulated Steichen. He studied for two weeks at an art academy, but the pedantic training did not hold his interest, so he returned to photography.

He longed to photograph Rodin, the great sculptor, and gave himself

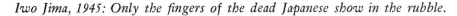

Iwo Jima, 1945: Only the fingers of the dead Japanese show in the rubble.

with intensity to the project, visiting the master every Saturday for a year. His photograph, "Rodin—Le Penseur," taken in 1902, won the best picture award at the International Exhibit in the Hague in 1904. His photography of illustrious people such as Rodin, Maurice Maeterlinck, the author, and Franz von Lenbach (the German painter) brought him a reputation; and by 1902, he was back in the States to open up a studio in New York City. He was famous, twenty-three years old, and soon was making portraits of the likes of J. P. Morgan and Eleonora Duse. He joined Stieglitz in 1905, helping establish the Photo-Secession Gallery; called "291," it exhibited art in all media—photography, painting, sculpture. Steichen personally was responsible for introducing Rodin, Cezanne, Matisse, John Marin, Gordon Craig, Brancusi and others to art lovers in the U. S. But by 1906, weary of commercial portraiture, he moved back to France, where, for several years, he painted, made photographs and began experimenting with the crossbreeding of plants.

From 1907 to 1917, Steichen seemed to have been in that period of evaluation one goes through who is indentured for life to art. He mixed with notable people such as Gertrude Stein, the American author, and John Marin; in France and in the States, he made some notable photographs—portraits of George Bernard Shaw, Henri Matisse, President Theodore Roosevelt; and nature studies, "Lotus, Mount Kisco," and "Frog on Lily Pads." He was helping artists—Cezanne and Picasso for example—gain recognition in America. In 1914, as the German Army advanced toward Paris, Edward Steichen returned to the U. S. again, there to work with Stieglitz at the Photo-Secession Gallery.

When the U. S. entered the war, Steichen decided to enlist; he had great feeling for his country and for France, his second mother country. He explained his purpose in *A Life in Photography:* "I wanted to be a photographic reporter, as Mathew Brady had been in the Civil War, and I went to Washington to offer my services, with the endorsement of the Camera Clubs of America." He was accepted by the Signal Corps, along with two other photographers, and they were given commissions as lieutenants. This was the beginning of his confrontation with war, and he would do as much as any photographer could to expose its awful waste and brutality. Years later, he said: "I've spent over six years of my life in uniform. That's quite an indictment of civilization. . . . War is a a monstrous piece of human stupidity. And I can't look at it any other way."

The thirty-eight-year-old officer-photographer was leaving part one of his apprenticeship, and, although he couldn't foresee it, his work would take a sharp new direction after World War I.

His training began in the States, where he was coached by a Major Campbell, an English aerial photographer. Then he was shipped to France and the British front to learn all he could about aerial photography. Convinced that he belonged with the Air Force, he wrangled a transfer from the Signal Corps to the Photographic Section of the Air Service, and moved to General Pershing's headquarters at Chaumont. Soon he was placed in charge of the photographic operation, where he showed great managerial ability, the ability to plan, to handle personnel and material, coordinating both for a smooth follow-through. American doughboys were moving up for their first fight with the Germans at the Second Battle of the Marne. General Billy Mitchell, America's spunky, outspoken air warrior, needed some big aerial cameras and turned to Edward Steichen, who had one delivered immediately. Before the Meuse-Argonne offensive he worked for the no-nonsense general again. Mitchell wanted a mobile photo section in a hurry, and Steichen's well-trained adjutant delivered the goods in the crisis. Steichen drove toward Argonne where, near the front, a photo team was working in the truck, developing film and printing pictures of the battle. They worked all night in the mobile lab, because they had thousands of negatives and had to make fifty prints of each one, and then distribute them to headquarters and to the front lines. At 7 A.M., Lieutenant Steichen left the lab to rustle up some breakfast for his hard-working crew. He met General Mitchell sauntering down the street. General Billy shot two sharp questions at Steichen: Was the truck and outfit there? Yes. When would the prints be ready?

"We delivered the first five thousand this morning," Steichen answered.

"Good," Mitchell said, and continued his walk. The processing and printing was a formidable job under pressure, and Steichen had won a friend in Billy Mitchell.

World War I, with its muddy, rat-infested trenches and bloody, over-the-top charges, was the most murderous war ever fought up to that time. Masses of men hurled themselves at each other, charging over fields speckled with barbed wire and pockmarked by thousands of shell holes. They fought with bayonets and sabers, hand to hand, for a few square yards of ground. At Verdun, the longest and bloodiest battle, in the year 1916 alone over 300,000 Frenchmen died; nearly three-quarters of the entire French Army served in the long campaign that lasted until August, 1917. And during the Meuse-Argonne, 120,000 Americans were killed or wounded. From 1914 to 1918, about eight and a half million soldiers were killed; and in the same period, over twelve million civilians died from military action, from starvation, disease and exposure due to the war.

When peace came on Nov. 11, 1918, Edward Steichen fell into a depression that lasted for days—a severe reaction to the wholesale death and devastation he had seen. Years later he recalled:

"I went into my room at the barracks and flung myself on the bed. The whole monstrous horror of the war seemed to fall down on me and smother me. I smelled the rotting carcasses of dead horses, saw the three white faces of the first American dead that I had seen. I could hear the rat-a-tat-tat of machine-gun fire as one lay on one's belly trying to dig into the earth to escape the fire, and the ping-pinging of the bullets coming through the leaves overhead. I saw the dried blood around the bullet hole in a young soldier's head. And he was only one of hundreds of thousands. How could men and nations have been so stupid? What was life for if it had to end like this? What was the use of living?"

Like many sensitive men of conscience Steichen felt guilt for his involvement in the war, although, in his role as photographic specialist, he had not personally killed a single soldier. He turned to art for consolation, vowing to make a positive contribution to mankind, to erase the pernicious war experience.

He remained in France, painting pictures of flowers, thinking and searching his soul, still not settled in his métier. One morning he found a picture—a copy of one of his own—in his studio. It was the work of his gardener, an untutored peasant, and was superior to Steichen's. He knew then that his career as a painter was over, and with dramatic flair, he called in the gardener. Together they hauled all his paintings into a clearing—and set fire to them!

He returned to his photographic apprenticeship and began to experiment, taking the kind of sharp and clear photographs that war had demanded. He began the now-famous project of photographing a white cup and saucer. This "finger exercise," as he called it, required several months and hundreds of negatives. He also experimented with various concepts, including an attempt to illustrate, symbolically, Einstein's Theory of Relativity. He failed; the pictures are meaningless to anyone but the photographer, who used symbols that only he understood. But photographs such as "Pears on a Plate," "A Bee on a Sunflower" and the renowned "Wheelbarrow with Flower Pots" retain a remarkable appeal, many years after they were made. They have a clarity and purpose that teach an implicit lesson to all photographers: the simple, pure image is the lasting one.

In 1923, his post-World War I appenticeship completed, Steichen entered the world of commerce as chief photographer for the Condé Nast publications in New York City. At that time, he was billed as "the greatest living portrait photographer," and was hired to shoot famous people and take occasional fashion photographs.

He pursued his new job with the zestfulness which is characteristic of all his enterprises and took a wide variety of commercial photographs—everything from matchboxes, tacks and spectacles and potatoes to evening gowns. It was that brand of photography—as it is indeed today—that has little chance of living beyond its time: clever, stagy and flashy, but flimsy. However, many of his portraits taken then still have impact. He photographed nearly everybody who was anybody—or who pretended to be: John Barrymore, Katherine Cornell, Lillian Gish, Paul Muni, Fred Astaire, Greta Garbo, Charlie Chaplin, and on and on. A few portraits —Winston Churchill, Willa Cather, Paul Robeson, Carl Sandburg—are strong yet, and this is remarkable if you consider how thin Steichen was spreading his talent. Busy as he was with commercial work for Condé Nast and advertising photography for the J. Walter Thompson agency, he still found time for "hobby" pictures—particularly the streets and buildings of New York.

He also made photographic illustrations for his daughter's book, *The First Picture Book: Everyday Things for Babies*, and for the Limited Edition Club's volume of Thoreau's *Walden*. From 1923 to 1938, when he "retired" from the mercantile rat race, he was undoubtedly

America's most famous cameraman—dynamic, prolific, a virtuoso. World War II brought him back to action. World War I, the "war to end all wars," had seared Steichen, although contributing to his creative direction. His feeling of disgust had not lessened, but he thought that photography, through honest imagery, might contribute toward making war obsolete. In 1941, at age sixty-two, he tried to enlist in the Air Force but was turned down because he was too old. After Pearl Harbor, the Navy offered him a commission as a Lieutenant Commander (USNR) to organize a team of photographers to record naval air activities. His photographic task force included Wayne Miller (later his assistant at The Museum of Modern Art), Charles Kerlee, Fenno Jacobs, Horace Bristol, Victor Jorgensen, Barrett Gallagher, John Swope, each of whom were commissioned by the Navy; also Willar Mace, a Navy Lieutenant, who served as executive assistant.

Steichen's cameramen came from a variety of fields, from journalism, documentary photography, illustration, advertising and marine photography. At first it was considered a motley crew by the regular Navy officers, who thought it undignified for fellow officers to carry cameras. But gradually Steichen's group won the admiration of the regular Navy men. Steichen sent them out on assignments, usually on carriers, and their instructions gave them the freedom to shoot as they saw fit, to photograph what happened, concentrating on the men involved. "The ships and planes will become obsolete, but the men will always be there," he told them.

In 1943, Edward Steichen and Lieutenant Victor Jorgensen shipped out on the carrier *Lexington*. In his book *The Blue Ghost* Steichen tells of his tour of duty aboard the "Lex." It is a microcosm of life at sea, of men under fire, weary to the bone but determined to prevail at all costs. Steichen and Jorgensen photographed the *Lexington* from stem to stern, capturing the elation and the anxiety of sailors and airmen, conveying the boredom and tension, and showing planes and ships in battle. The *Lexington* was in hot action during the Gilbert and Marshall Islands campaign, during which it was under air attack by Japanese bombers and torpedo planes. The planes struck savagely, in waves, over a seven-hour period and a torpedo damaged the carrier's rudder, so that the ship traveled in circles until repairs could be made on the propeller, which was used to steer the ship back to Pearl Harbor. The *Lexington* then returned to the States to be completely overhauled.

Steichen made one more mission into a combat area, arriving on Iwo Jima a day after the island was secured by American forces. There he made a powerful photograph of a dead Japanese, covered by rubble—except for his curled fingers protruding from the debris.

Before war's end, Captain Edward Steichen was in charge of all naval combat photography, and had done yeoman service, including the supervision of a movie, *The Fighting Lady*, and two exhibitions at The Museum of Modern Art: "Road to Victory" and "Power in the Pacific." (The latter was published as a book, as was another collection called "U. S. Navy War Photographs.") The exhibitions were powerful (Carl Sandburg, Steichen's brother-in-law, wrote captions for "Road to Victory"): they were the first exhibits on a large scale to use photographs to dramatize a theme. They were another demonstration of Steichen's skill as an organizer of men and material; thousands of photographs had to be screened to get 150 prints for "Power in the Pacific"; captions had to be written, blowups made and hung to make a coherent story. The exhibitions were excellent, the conception of a superb showman and producer, Edward Steichen. Fine as they were, though, they were merely the prelude to a greater exhibit to come—an exhibit which would gain their producer a reputation as the world's finest photo editor.

World War II added another leaf to his apprenticeship and fortified his antiwar attitude. In 1947, his career took a new direction when he became Director of the Department of Photography at The Museum of Modern Art in New York City. For the next fifteen years he directed, with dramatic zest, numerous exhibitions, seeking to make the public aware of the power and stature of photography. The first exhibit included the work of three photojournalists: Wayne Miller, with a series on the birth of his son; Leonard McCombe's documentation of war refugees; and Homer Page's commentary on an American Legion convention. All in all, he organized forty-four exhibitions of serious photographers at work in the U. S., Europe and Japan, including old-timers and

77

contemporary cameramen. In his third attempt to dramatize the stupidity of war, he produced an exhibition on the Korean war, which he considered had been more realistically interpreted than any previous war. Dominating the exhibit were the powerful photographs by David Douglas Duncan.

"People flocked in great numbers to see it," Steichen recalled. "They found some pictures revolting, some deeply moving. There were even tears shed, but that was as far as it went. They left the exhibition and promptly forgot it."

He had failed again to arouse people so they would protest collectively the futility of war in our time. He concluded that his approach was wrong—too negative—and what was needed was a positive approach, "on what a wonderful thing life was, how marvelous people were, and, above all, how alike people were in all parts of the world."

This was the seed for perhaps the most awesome photographic exhibition ever attempted: its theme, "The Family of Man," was drawn from a speech by Abraham Lincoln. Conceived as a mirror of the brotherhood of man, it required nearly three years, a screening of two million photographs from sixty-eight countries; until, finally, there were 503 photographs, the work of 273 men and women, renowned and unknown photographers. In a preliminary survey, Steichen visited eleven countries to find out if his concept was feasible. It was. Work began; assistants were lined up; a loft in an old building was rented for a work area and to house the flood of pictures. Although Steichen was the catalyst, and worked desperately hard on the project, he gave Wayne Miller, his chief assistant, a great deal of credit for the success of the venture. (Miller personally screened some two million photographs, a marathon and, one imagines, exhausting performance.)

The Family of Man was a huge success, breaking all attendance records for exhibitions of contemporary works at The Museum of Modern Art. It opened in 1955 and by 1963 had been viewed by over nine million people in sixty-nine countries. Steichen personally visited seven cities in four countries, including Moscow, where the exhibition opened in 1959. In book form, *The Family of Man* has sold over 2,500,000 copies since 1955. Its photographs of men, women and children in their everyday activities, from birth to death, are tender and eloquent—a testimonial to Edward Steichen's concern for humanity, a kind of summing up of his case for a sane world.

Painter and photographer, editor and showman—artist, craftsman, teacher—Steichen retired in 1962 from his directorship at The Museum of Modern Art. In celebration of his eighty-second birthday, the Museum had given him a one-man show of his photos in 1961—three hundred pictures from his collection of thirty thousand negatives. In October, 1962, the Museum opened an exhibit Steichen had thought about for years. It was called "The Bitter Years" and documented the plight of rural America, 1935–1941, as seen by Roy Stryker's photographers working for the Farm Security Administration.

Although Edward Steichen is officially retired, he is unofficially very active with his first love, photography. Across a pond in the back yard of his home in Connecticut there is a lovely shadblow tree. He has been photographing it for years, from season to season, at various times of day, in all kinds of weather. He began with a still camera but switched to motion pictures to give the story the continuity of rain and wind, of chirping birds and croaking frogs. He visualized this as a "photographic cencerto," and expects to finish it soon.

Thus, the apprenticeship that began over seventy years ago continues. Photography, in all forms and facets, is a way of life for Edward Steichen.

In 1908, Auguste Rodin came to Steichen's home to give him a present, a lovely bronze statue called "The Walking Man." It was first created in 1877, but a bronze casting was not made until years later. Rodin saw his creation as a symbol and tribute to Steichen's creative destiny—"a continuous marching onward." Of course, tributes have been heaped upon Steichen—the Presidential Medal of Freedom, honorary degrees and decorations—but "The Walking Man" is the most fitting, for it truly symbolizes the restless virtuosity of this extraordinary man— a charter member in the family of man.

Carl Mydans, photographer and writer.

Carl Mydans

A Korean mother and her baby flee Seoul, 1951. (Life photos by Carl Mydans)

Korea, 1950: A compassionate American carriers a wounded GI.

3. The Mind and the Hand

CARL MYDANS is that rare person whose body and mind are synchronized by a sense of purpose. Deeply motivated and dedicated, he has roamed the world for over thirty years, recording history as it happens: Depression in the U. S., war in Europe and Asia, peace and prosperity and reconstruction—then more war in Korea, more struggle and devastation. These turbulent events have etched his face with experience, and his warm, alert eyes are quick to mirror compassion. There is a steadiness in his gaze and manner—the steadiness of a man in control of himself—that suggests a difficult man to shake. A short, sturdy man with the hands of a craftsman—a cabinetmaker or a surgeon—he might have been successful at either career. Instead, he chose journalism, committing himself to action and involvement, to wading with sandhogs on a river bottom, climbing high above a bridge, and slogging through the mud and dust of war. These experiences would broaden an inquisitive mind and deepen a sensibility responsive to the greatness of man under stress. And the images of war, on battlefields and in prison camps—particularly the faces of suffering, enduring people—would shape a view of life based on love of mankind. He would excel as a writer-photographer for *Life* magazine and, in a procession of events, become a superb human being.

Born on May 20, 1907, in Boston, Massachusetts, he is a first-generation American whose ancestors fled Russia to escape war and the terror of endless pogroms. His father, David Mydans, the son of a bookbinder who lived near Odessa, quickly discarded the ways of the Old World for the intoxicating challenge of the new one. His mother—with the poetic first name of Leah—had fine creative instincts, which she channeled into homemaking pursuits such as cooking and crocheting. The family was warm and well-knit, a stimulating environment for the growth of talent and intellect.

The Mydanses settled in Medford, Massachusetts, a picturesque community on the meandering Mystic River. The childhood of Carl Mydans was happy, almost idyllic, and tinged by the romance of the sea. Medford was a small town, secure and comfortable, perhaps a little sleepy and complacent, like so many American communities before World War I. Growing up in the cradle of the American Revolution—not far from Lexington and Concord, close to Bunker Hill and the Boston Common—young Carl was deeply patriotic. *This* was his native land, and he was intensely aware of its heritage. He developed a sense of history. He had a sense of place, a rootedness, that would remain with him for years and fortify him in moments of crisis.

He was stirred by the mystique of shipbuilding and by the legends of the clipper ships. Small boats were being built in Mystic in those days, but occasionally a four-master could be seen on the tidal river, heading for far-off lands and setting a boy's fancy adrift. When he was thirteen, he went to work part-time in a boatyard. He learned to handle tools—the saw, the plane, the hammer—and how to calk the seam of a boat. He enjoyed working with his hands and became proud of doing a job with skill and precision. His boss, a fine New Englander named Bob Cheney, taught him to seek perfection and to set high personal standards. Carl remembers those days with deep affection and appreciation. "There is no more wonderful place for a child to grow up than around a boatyard in New England," he said years later.

So he dreamed of becoming a shipbuilder, a noble, creative profession with a lore that was enchanting. Later on, he visited a hospital in Boston; the sight of a surgeon at work struck him with awe. He bestowed upon the surgeon's hands the same reverence he had given the hands of a joiner, or those of his father as he played the oboe in the family parlor. He would become a surgeon, he thought, and perform godlike operations. But this was a passing notion and faded when he discovered his true profession, which he wrote of in his autobiography, *More Than Meets the Eye:*

Sometime during my last years of high school, journalism caught my imagination . . . And I have since credited myself with selecting the most satisfying and exciting of professions, for in the pursuit of journalism, perhaps more than any other profession, one comes closer to and lives more intimately and imaginatively with the world he loves. This is especially true of photojournalism; for here one joins mind and hand, and here the reporter must always come in closest contact with his subject.

His early zest has never left him, for, like all great reporters, he has a profound sense of urgency as immediate and pressing as a teletype. He whetted his appetite for journalism in high school when he began working for a local newspaper as a "stringer." Later on, he sold copy by the inch, a typical practice of the time. At Boston University, he was a reporter, desk editor and, finally, associate news editor of the *Boston University News*. He graduated in 1930 with a B. S. in Journalism, and worked as a free-lance writer for the Boston *Herald* and the Boston *Globe*. Next, he took his first staff job for the *American Banker*, where he began using a camera, realizing its potential as a tool for communication. The mind and the hand were about to merge, for Carl Mydans would soon play a role in one of the most significant creative projects undertaken in the United States.

In 1935, he put down the typewriter (temporarily) and picked up the camera full-time, joining the photographic unit of the Resettlement Administration within the Department of Agriculture (which later was merged into the Farm Security Administration Photographic Unit). The nation was mired in the Great Depression, and the story needed to be told with graphic clarity. It was a story of lands blowing away and people drifting in grim poverty, despairing of help and approaching desperation. Roy Stryker, a perceptive educator and editor, organized a task force of gifted photographers to tour the nation and interpret it through the shape of the land and in the faces of the unemployed, the migrants, the sharecroppers, the dispossessed. Among the group were great documentarians such as Dorothea Lange, Walker Evans and Russell Lee; the fine artist Ben Shahn; the brilliant Arthur Rothstein, now Technical Director of Photography at *Look* magazine; and Carl Mydans.

At this stage in his career, Mydans was fortunate indeed to become involved in this great undertaking—and to come under the tutelage of Stryker, a great teacher and catalyst. "Stryker could inspire a man," Mydans once said, looking back in gratitude. "He excited you about America, about recording history taking place. He gave you an awareness of your role as a photographer. And he insisted that you know the subject thoroughly before aiming a camera."

Mydans learned. He learned about cotton, about flood control and submarginal farming, about rural electrification, about beef and dairy cattle. He saw the faces of people, and he felt the helplessness of the parents and the flicker of hope in the eyes of children. He learned to put feeling on film, with simplicity and honesty—using light and shadow for mood, showing character by the lines in a face or the glint in the eyes. He learned the craft of the photo essay, the use of a series of pictures to tell a story. He became a photojournalist, and a photojournalist with a social conscience. He added a new dimension to his love of country, cultivating a fascination for farming, so that he now says, "I am a vicarious farmer." He added a "plank" to his photographic platform: "To understand the world around you, you have to know what's happening in your own country. If you are going to photograph farming in Yugoslavia, you had better understand it in America—if you are an American photographer—or in Sweden, if you're Swedish."

If the Farm Security Administration was like a Master of Arts degree for Carl Mydans, then his next experience was equivalent to a Ph.D. In 1936, he joined the staff of an exciting new publication, *Life*. It was a dynamic environment and made a vivid impression on him, as he wrote in *More Than Meets the Eye:*

One scene keeps coming back to me from those early days on *Life:* there was a large room called the bull pen filled with desks and heaped with books and papers, pictures and charts and maps. Young men and women sat among them telephoning, reading, talking, typewriting. An editor came in. "Anyone here an expert on brain surgery?" he asked.

There was a moment's silence and then a young reporter tore the paper out of his typewriter. "Not yet," he replied, turning to the telephone, "but give me ten minutes and I will be."

Mydans was swept up in the current of events, in a dizzy dash from assignment to assignment—portraits of Congressmen and cowboys, photographs of strikes, of Hollywood movie-making and High Mass at St. Peter's Cathedral. "In these first few years," he wrote in his autobiography, "I had no home at all. All places were alike to me: all stimulating, all exciting and full of people and things to be seen and photographed."

Then he met Shelley Smith, a lovely writer and researcher on the *Life* staff. They were married in June, 1938, and a year later went abroad as a writer-photographer team, the first roving correspondents *Life* sent overseas. For the next six years, Carl, with Shelley sometimes at his side, roved from bombed-out city to battlefield to prison camp to battlefield—London under siege, Finland at bay, France in retreat, the chaos of China, the fall of Manila. Clashing armies, streams of refugees, bombers overhead, tanks moving up, weary men bowed under heavy packs. "We have lived a generation of wars," he said recently, "and I was involved in most of them."

His first look at combat came in Finland, when the brave little nation fought massive Russian armies in the winter snows. His report of the massacre of a Russian army at Kemi River was the first major text and photo essay on war ever published by *Life* (January 29, 1940). The battle was eerie and made a profound impression on him.

It was fought in the far north in temperatures of 22 degrees below zero, through forests of snow and ice. A Russian division had invaded Finland, a single column, including two tanks, carts, foot soldiers, men in sleighs and riding Mongolian ponies. The quick-moving Finns blew the tracks off the lead tank and the tank at the rear of the column, isolating the invaders and then cutting them to pieces. The trapped Russians, dazed by the onslaught and paralyzed by intense cold and fear, died in the dark, northern night, falling and freezing stiff like slabs of wood. Broken trucks and overturned sleighs lined the road. Men and horses lay side by side. Strings of bologna, slices of black bread, shattered helmets, gas masks, tins of tobacco, broken harnesses, shells, cans of tuna fish—chaos everywhere. And three thousand dead Russians.

"I have never got over that scene," Mydans told the author. "I have seen many other battlefields since, but none has left such an imprint on my mind as that winter night in Finland. There were so many dead. It

87

was such a far-away area, you know. North of the Arctic Circle. Remote. And it all seemed a kind of fantasy with men garbed in outlandish winter clothing, battling in horrendous cold."

Photographing the war in Finland was depressing in an incongruous way. The snow was a beautiful mantle, like a postcard of a New England winter. The ground crunched crisply underfoot; the trees were festooned with icicles. But beneath the blanket of fresh snow lay dead men frozen in grotesque positions. It was an extremely dangerous and difficult environment for a photographer. At Lake Ladoga, Mydans was nearly killed by a stick of bombs falling directly at him from the sky.

The sub-zero temperatures could freeze a camera's shutter, so he carried his two Contax cameras under a heavy sheepskin coat. To make a picture, he had to whip out one of them, remove his gloves, focus and shoot quickly. Although he got his fingers frostbitten, his photographs were sharp and clear, revealing, with starkness, war at first hand.

One touching series showed the sadness and terror of civilians under air attack. In early February, 1940, the village of Tammisaari became a ghost town every day from dawn to dark. Before the waves of Russian planes made their bombing runs, all activity stopped and old men, women and children hid in the fir and birch forest. They huddled around fires, gossiping, playing games and eating what food was available. Mydans showed them cowering on the frozen earth, clutching each other and staring helplessly at the sky.

Finland fell. Carl Mydans went to Italy to cover Fascism, on to France to witness its defeat, to Pearl Harbor to photograph American naval operations and then to China, in December, 1940. He and Shelley were to report on China's struggle against the Japanese, whose forces threatened Asia from Manchuria to Indochina. The Mydanses' headquarters were in the war-time capital of Chungking, which the enemy was trying to bomb into submission. In the months to follow, the peripatetic Mydanses traveled deep into the heart of China, to Lanchow, the capital of Kansu province and to Tungkwan, whose ancient fort guarded the Yellow River. In the fall of 1941, they headed south to Malaya to do a story on Singapore, the bastion of Western defense, and from there, in mid-October, to Manila. Less than two months after their arrival, the

Philippines were overrun and the Mydanses imprisoned by the Japanese.

A prisoner of war camp is a crucible for the human character. Integrity and decency are challenged by privation and by the sheer fact of confinement, which breeds boredom, depression, despair and, too often, cowardice. Weak, selfish people sell out their friends for small favors, for extra food and tobacco and other special privileges. Since hope is the foundation for enduring, false hope is generated by rumor. In 1942, at the Santo Tomas camp in Manila, the prisoners' dream of freedom was linked to the vision of American military power, personified by General Douglas MacArthur. At this time, of course, America's military power was weak and MacArthur had few men and little material to supply them.

The prisoners of Santo Tomas maintained their sanity and increased their chances of survival by building a democratic community within the walls. They organized a government, hospital facilities, a school, a police force; they improved the plumbing and heating; they pitched in to do the manual work essential to daily living. Carl Mydans mopped the floor of the hospital and carried bedpans for sick patients. His only opportunity to use a camera came when the Japanese commandant named Tsurumi summoned him to his office. With the commandant were two officers, one a full colonel in elegant attire. Mydans described the scene in *More Than Meets the Eye:*

"The colonel has just had a report about you," began Tsurumi, laughing nervously. "He says you are a famous photographer. He has seen your pictures of China in *Life*. He has come to give you a camera and take you out of camp so that you may continue your professional work."

The Japanese wanted him to photograph a victory parade in Manila, offering to free him and Shelley if he would accept. Carl Mydans refused this attempt to use his name and talent for propaganda purposes. He explained that their countries were at war and that if he took pictures for them he would forever be a man without a country, just as a Japanese prisoner would be dishonored and disowned if he worked for the American Army.

89

At this the colonel suddenly rose and without waiting for Tsurumi's translation said in English, "I see. I see." Then he bowed slightly and looked at me. "I understand," he said. "You may go." And I was dismissed.

Although photographic expression was impossible in a concentration camp, another, more passive, form of creativity—that of observing and feeling and thinking—could be developed. Understanding was deepened, sympathy quickened and compassion enlarged through participation in the common endurance of confinement. Being a prisoner of war is a profound experience, and if a man survived and maintained his equilibrium, he could add dimension to his insight. In his autobiography, Carl Mydans showed a maturity of thought worthy of a fine novelist (the prison camp episode echoes of E. E. Cummings' superb *The Enormous Room*, a dramatization of life in a World War I prison camp).

More Than Meets the Eye, a subjective title, suggested an impatience with the pure objectivity of a camera lens. Mydans seemed to be saying that beneath the stream of events—like fine silt on a murky river bottom —are elusive nuances impossible to capture on film. His descriptions of the prisoner of war camp, sprinkled with quicksilver anecdotes and observations, reveal a mind aware of human folly—a mind capable of irony and humor as well as tender concern. The Japanese were as imprisoned as their captives, he implies, both trapped by circumstances, pawns of a larger game—war.

Captivity gave Carl Mydans a new layer of experience, perhaps the ultimate coat of maturity, so that when he was repatriated in 1943 his mind and hand were completely wedded to the events and people of his time. He and Shelley came back to an America that was booming with purpose, turning out guns, tanks, planes and trained men and women, united in resolution to end World War II. Soon he was back at the front, trudging with infantrymen into the battle of Cassino and following them along the road to Rome. From Italy he went to Marseilles to cover the fighting in southern France, and then rushed back to the South Pacific, to be with MacArthur and his troops on their triumphant return

to the Philippines.

It was a moment to savor. In January, 1945, Carl Mydans stood on the quarterdeck of the cruiser *Boise*, the flagship of the invasion fleet sailing for Luzon. As he talked with General MacArthur he could see on the watery horizon the line that marked Bataan. Three weeks after the invasion of Lingayen, Carl Mydans joined seven hundred men of the 8th Cavalry Regiment for a two-day sixty-mile blitzkrieg charge into Manila. The objective: Santo Tomas prison and the speedy liberation of four thousand people held captive for three years. For Mydans, returning to his former "home" with the rampaging liberators, the experience had to be joy and jubilation and vindication all rolled into one. He looked upon his old friends with loving, paternalistic eyes, for they were about to feel the elation of freedom he had savored upon his repatriation. He joined them again, sharing the same chow line, walking with them in the compound, talking over the old days and soothing their apprehensions about returning to the "outside world"—for all prisoners have this anxiety. The war was grinding to a close; everybody sensed that, and the liberation of Santo Tomas was the first celebration of the end of a long struggle.

When the Japanese surrendered in August, 1945, Carl Mydans went in with the occupation forces, and shortly thereafter he and Shelley took up residence in Tokyo. Carl became chief of the Time-Life news bureau and the Mydanses settled down to raise a family (a boy, Seth Anthony, was born in 1947 and a girl, Shelley, in 1949). For Carl, life was comparatively quiet, except for three events: he was in the middle of the earthquake at Fukui—one of the worst in the history of Japan; he covered some of the Communist revolution in China; and he saw how the Viet Minh fought the French in Indochina. But another big war was brewing for the United States, and Mydans would soon be in the middle of it.

He was in New York in June, 1950, when word flashed out from Korea that war had begun. Ten days later, transported into battle so quickly that events blurred before his eyes, he was walking along a muddy road, following young Americans north to the danger and death of the Yalu River. In its July 7 issue, *Life* announced in a headline, "Mydans Goes Up to the Fighting." He was at the front again, one of the great war photographers of all time, to cover the men on foot, to sleep alongside them and to share their moments of suffering in an alien, hostile land. Again, the familiar pictures of tired faces and churning machines and the trenchant prose comments: with the 1st Cavalry as they landed at P'ohang-dong; with them at Yondong to relieve the 24th Division, as they fought and backed up and buried their comrades; watching refugees wading a river while fighting men waved them along with impatient gestures. "The despair on their faces was familiar. I had seen it in Finland, France, in China," he cabled; with MacArthur during the landing at Inchon; with *Life* photographers David Duncan and Hank Walker as the Army fought from house-to-house at Seoul.

In 1950, Carl Mydans received a Gold Achievement Award from *U. S. Camera* for his reportage of the Korean War. "His photographs and cabled reports have produced a new type of pictorial reportage in which has been blended photographic and editorial craftsmanship of highest caliber," went the citation in part.

The war photographs of Carl Mydans are intimate and warm, showing not only a deep involvement with events but with the men who make them. In them is a sense of history personally felt, and it is pointless to attempt further description. Look them up in *Life* magazine and see the radiance of human spirit. A man took them, a man who knows where he stands and what his lifework is all about, a man who can state his purpose clearly, without sham or self-consciousness:

A war correspondent cannot function unless he is part of the unit he is covering. A photographer's job, like that of a writer, is to record history. He must never forget this. It is so important, so all pervasive, that it has carried me through the terror of combat. . . . When I've said—as others have said—in a very tough spot: "What am I doing here?" I've always found comfort and the will to go on in my own answer. My job is to record the history of our times.

What is the role of the war photographer? Where does his allegiance lie in a war which may seem to have dubious value? There is a simple answer, Mydans says:

If you are a reporter, you cover what is happening. You must. It is your job. I cannot say to myself I will cover only what is good, or what is bad. An honest presentation of what I see and feel is all I can hope for.

But it shouldn't be supposed that a war correspondent by his presence and action in reporting a war condones the violence of war. A photographer has a choice at certain times of taking a picture or participating, of choosing between his historic function and his human one. There is a conflict. Each must make his choice. Suppose a tank has been hit, catches fire, and men are struggling to get out. Do you make pictures of it? Or do you help the people out? An experienced man weighs it quickly—and makes his decision. If on an assault landing men called for aid and assistance—it's up to the photographer to decide whether to make pictures or help them. I have never known a good war photographer who was not a deeply compassionate man and who did not make his decision in such a circumstance on the side of compassion.

"After thirty-five every man is responsible for his own face." So wrote the great French author Albert Camus. The face of Carl Mydans shows the side he has chosen—the side of compassion.

David Douglas Duncan, Korea, 1950.

David Douglas Duncan

4. Vagabond at War

DAVID DOUGLAS DUNCAN, who hails from the heartland of America, is the cheerful nomad of photojournalism. For the past thirty years, he has been in global pursuit of pictures, ranging with relentless goodwill from the Americas to Asia and Europe, and back again. He is a shy, soft-spoken man whose self-reliance and resolution generate respect and, perhaps, a stab of envy. You cannot help admire such an adventuresome character; and envy for his successful tumbleweed career is softened by understanding its hardships and dangers. He has seen death close up many times, in World War II and in Korea and

U. S. Marines, 1950, Korea: Photographed by David Douglas Duncan.

Palestine; his book *This Is War* is one of the most intense photographic documents of combat ever produced. An "old-fashioned" rugged individualist, he is a one-man corporation who produces his handsome, expensive books—*The Private World of Pablo Picasso, The Kremlin, Picasso's Picassos, Yankee Nomad*—from idea to printed page and then sells the distribution rights. This "corporate individualism" requires steely determination and the ability to work like a Missouri mule, the two prime characteristics of this Midwestern vagabond.

Born in Kansas City, Missouri, in 1916, David Duncan had a happy childhood and a carefree attitude toward school. Early in life he showed his freedom-loving, independent nature: on the way to his first day in school he broke away from his mother and crossed the street by himself. Recalling the episode years later, he remarked, "I never liked anyone to take me anywhere."

As a twelve-year-old, he sometimes skipped school to go hunting in the river bottoms south of the city—and he loved to sit on the roof of the Duncan house and bang away at blackbirds with a shotgun! He was a prankster who often got caught in the act and was punished; with a devilish flourish, he protested one punishment by setting fire to a family table cloth. In his autobiography, *Yankee Nomad*, he wrote: "Throughout childhood it was always I who was caught, especially at Bryant School, where I was expelled so often that my presence in class for a full unbroken month was considered rather unusual."

He was a born adventurer, a Tom Sawyer, who had deep affection for his parents and siblings. The Duncan family was warm and lively; there were four other children—a sister and three brothers. The father, Kenneth Duncan, was a genial entrepreneur who owned a lumber company that failed in the 1920s. He was adventuresome in a stay-at-home, business way; when one venture failed, he immediately plunged into another. After his lumber business went broke, he founded a theater corporation made up of three movie houses in Kansas City. He operated like a neighborhood Santa Claus, giving away, on bonus nights, plump turkeys, Oriental rugs, excellent china and silverware, to the point that the gifts devoured the profits.

Young Dave brought piles of friends to the movies free of charge. He
wrote in *Yankee Nomad:* "On Saturday afternoons as a kid I used to

fill entire streetcars with schoolmates and, by running between perform-ances hit all three shows starting with the two o'clock matinee at the first, ending with the seven o'clock matinee at the last. . . . I grandiosely handed out boxes of popcorn as we climbed into our tiers of seats." The generosity of father and son, coupled with the decline of silent films, soon put the Duncans out of business and compelled new enterprises.

Growing up in Kansas City, he dreamed of becoming an archaeologist. After high school, he enrolled at the University of Arizona, where, in 1934, he had his first brush with his true career. Early one January morning, the largest hotel in Tucson caught fire and Duncan, almost as an afterthought, ran to the scene carrying a thirty-nine-cent camera. Outside the burning building, he took two photographs of a half-dressed, excited man who kept trying to sneak back into the hotel to retrieve his suitcase. Those were the first photos Duncan ever made, and the next day he read in the newspaper that his subject had been the notorious John Dillinger. Since he hadn't bothered to get the film developed, he missed a chance for a "scoop." But he would seldom miss that kind of oppor-tunity in the years of photography that lay ahead; for he would prove to be a natural reporter who loved to be at the center of action.

About two years after the Dillinger episode, Duncan transferred to the University of Miami, where he studied zoology and Spanish. His Florida friends were tough, earthy characters, prizefighters (Duncan was a good amateur boxer), deep-sea divers, a bookie, a cop and Ross Allen, the reptile expert, with whom Duncan explored the tropical wilds. He devoted his summers to diving for salvage on the sunken vessels off the Florida keys. And he began to sharpen his camera eye, during school terms and on vacation. As an amateur photographer, he was almost a stereotype of the "photo bug" who prowls the streets and fields with camera always at hand, taking pictures of pretty girls, friends, strangers and stray cats. Somewhere along the way—perhaps when he won two hundred and fifty dollars in a national snapshot contest—he decided to become a photojournalist. After graduating with a Bachelor of Arts degree in 1938, he began his nomadic career, heading south in pursuit of fun and excitement.

His early quests are a profile of the universal picaresque youth: wan-derings in Central and South America—in desert, jungle, upon the ocean.

But beneath the surface tones of romance and wanderlust—echoed in his "Gee-whiz what-fun" letters to the folks at home—was the seriousness of a dedicated craftsman. There was a deep feeling for nature in his work, a rapport with wind and water, with birds and fish and animals. His photographs of Mexican plowmen and Cayman Islanders show a remarkable maturity and objectivity for a young man. He particularly admired those proud, quiet fishermen engaged in the ancient struggle with the sea. He lived with them as a shipmate, melting into their environment as only a born reporter can, and then freezing their daily life on film. His portraits of their faces—clear and direct—are warm little studies by an artisan who respects men who work with their hands, close to the elemental world—the capricious ocean and wild winds.

Duncan's down-to-earth, on-the-levelness is a gift that cannot be faked. He is without pretension or affectation. It shines through his personality, in his steady, understated confidence, in his unassuming style. It enables him to get close to fishermen, soldiers, farmers and tribesmen and to worldly characters such as Pablo Picasso.

Bouncing about in southern climes, Dave Duncan skirted bankruptcy by selling photos—sometimes at three dollars each—to a variety of markets: the Milwaukee *Journal*, Baltimore *Sun*, Cleveland *Plain Dealer*, Chicago *Tribune*, *Family Circle*. The St. Louis *Post-Dispatch* paid him ten dollars for a black and white photograph and twenty-five for color (a high rate for a newspaper rotogravure section in those days). He also sold to the *National Geographic*, which admired the honesty and authenticity of his work. In 1940, he was a member of an expedition, sponsored by Michael Lerner, to catch broadbill swordfish for the American Museum of Natural History. On this oceangoing safari, he became the first man ever to photograph the giant killer squid of the Humboldt Current. However, his experiences weren't always so scientific; in fact, they often seemed like something out of a hoked-up adventure story—but were always true.

In 1942, while driving a car through the boondocks of Mexico he was ambushed by bandits. About a dozen hard-looking hombres armed to the teeth stopped the car he was driving through the wild mountains. They pointed their pistols and rifles at Duncan and his two friends and commented to one another about the spoils and how to share them.

Duncan and his companions, a young American couple, knew Spanish, but the photographer immediately began speaking English, to throw the *bandidos* off stride. One of the gang knew a little English and began a discussion, to impress his chief and comrades. Duncan encouraged the man, who poked his head into the car and chattered away in a babble of drunken words. Meanwhile, the car motor was idling and Duncan was waiting for the chance to grind the gas pedal to the floor and take off. When the opportunity arose, the photographer stomped on the accelerator, flicking off the headlights as the car shot ahead. With his left arm he put a choke-hold on the English-speaking bandit, then shoved him head over heels into the mesquite. The car bounded down the dark mountain road, throwing up a screen of dust between the *Americanos* and the startled highwaymen. Dave Duncan was delighted that he didn't have to use the Colt .38 pistol that lay next to his leg on the car seat.

By late 1942, Duncan's colorful adventures encompassed big-game hunting in the Canadian Rockies, romance with the beautiful lady bull-fighter Conchita Cintrón, amusing escapades with the pistol-packing president of Nicaragua, Anastasio Somoza, and various minor heroics and rescues—in short, enough action to enrich the average lifetime. But for the tall, carefree photographer, this was merely the end of the first act of the play. On February 17, 1943, he entered the U. S. Marine Corps. He was as prepared for war as anybody can be; a self-reliant, superbly conditioned man, all he needed to become a great combat photographer was the experience of battle—and a slice of luck.

Dave Duncan, like Margaret Bourke-White and Robert Capa, is one of those people who pursue action, attacking and challenging life itself, so that for them luck is merely "the residue of design." Commissioned as a second lieutenant, he considered himself lucky to become a Marine and then doubly fortunate to wind up as a specialist in the aviation arm, a small, select group of Marines. The fact that he landed in the group—he was a natural for it—indicates that military personnel procedures may not have been as capricious as most veterans contend. He won an Expert's Medal with a Colt .45 automatic and went through training easily (it was a waltz for such a jungle crawler), his only complaint being that little individual thinking was demanded. In September, 1943, he was shipped to the Pacific THEATER OF OPERATIONS to command a photo lab, 101 but by November he wangled a transfer to more active duty as a combat cameraman.

Detached from regular duty, Lt. Duncan floated about the Pacific to document Marine Corps aviation. It was like his free-lance days in South America; given freedom to move as he saw fit, his assignment was perhaps the first of its kind in the history of the Corps. His traveling orders, issued by South Pacific Combat Air Transport Command, undoubtedly were the envy of the entire Pacific THEATER OF OPERATIONS. He was given *carte blanche* to go where and when he had to, and to photograph whatever and whoever were necessary.

To photograph parachute drops from SCAT planes at Bougainville, Duncan was flown in a tiny Army plane to an outpost deep behind the lines. There he photographed—and fought alongside—fierce Fijian guerrillas and tough New Zealanders. The fire-fights were murderous nightmares; mortars, grenades, machine guns and small arms ripped through the bush as Fijians ambushed powerful Japanese forces. In one afternoon, more than one hundred Japanese were annihilated. The guerrillas, hidden in trees, behind logs, camouflaged by foliage, poured lead at the advancing enemy who, terrified by the dark jungle itself, were cut to pieces. As rain fell and the enemy charged in blurry waves, the guerrillas fell back, hurling grenades; and one huge Fijian—six-feet-seven-inches tall—stood flat-footed, firing a mortar from the waist. The first Fiji Battalion escaped the superior forces without loss of a single guerrilla. From this little-recalled battle came the legend of the "black ghosts" of the Solomons—a legend told throughout the Pacific.

Duncan drifted throughout the Pacific like a warrior troubador, often carrying an accordion, even though he couldn't play a single song. One is tempted to think that he saw himself in the role of an ancient bard, who might soothe the troubled troops if only he had the time to learn a tune. Yet battle was his scene and fighting men his friends and subjects. As one of the crew, he shared their hardships, danger and fear. Once, flying with a bomber over the East China Sea, he escaped death by an inch and wound up with a photograph made by a bizarre happening. As the Privateer bomber banked to strafe an attack-transport, it was hit by antiaircraft, but managed to return to base. The next day, the photographer discovered a small fragment of shell curled about the trigger guard of his Colt .45, which he normally carried in a holster under his left arm. As the plane lurched, the pistol had shifted forward, covering his heart and deflecting a piece of flack. Then, when Duncan developed the film in his camera, he found a picture of the enemy ship, taken before the bombing run could be made. He had not triggered the shutter; it had been tripped by the concussion of the Japanese shellfire. The enemy had made its own portrait.

Australia, Guam, Okinawa, the Philippines, Japan—Duncan, the gypsy Marine, went the route, including the surrender ceremonies on the U. S. S. *Missouri*. He made difficult and unusual pictures. Once he flew in a plastic "nose" tank strapped beneath the left wing of a P-38 fighter. It was a "tingling" sensation, he wrote in *Yankee Nomad*, coming down at 100 m.p.h., "with my nose seemingly an inch off the ground and about to plow that steel-gird runway from end to end." Another time he photographed an act of treason by a Japanese officer who guided Marine bombers on an air strike against his comrades. Duncan took portraits of the pitiful little man crouched in the waist of a bomber as it attacked the Japanese headquarters.

World War II was Duncan's final training for photographic renown; he acquired a knowledge of tactics and strategy and, more significant, the rapport with combat men that made possible his brilliant coverage of the Korean War. He became a Marine; indentured by battle into that permanent fraternity, the Corps, he was proud of their courage and understood their mystique. Yet he did not sacrifice a sliver of his independence, nor did service make him long for the rooted life of the Midwest. At war's end, he was as fiddle-footed as ever, his eye open for new fields where fresh entries could be made in his photographic journal.

One could write a fictionalized biography of a photojournalist by studying his passport and magazine credit lines, linking the two to current events. Then, if it were possible to analyze all the pictures the photographer ever took—thousands and thousands of images, most of which are never published—a writer could add depth to the characterization.* For

---

* For his autobiography, *Yankee Nomad*, which contains 500 photographs, Duncan edited a half million negatives. The collection represents 30 years of work; and the final selection— 1/10 of one percent of his total production. A magazine photographer is fortunate indeed if one percent of the pictures taken on any given assignment are published. The remainder are as invisible as the perennial iceberg beneath the sea.

you can read the mind of a photojournalist by studying his contact sheets, those little visual "notes" he makes for a story. Each roll of film is printed on a single sheet so that an editor, peering through a magnifying glass or special viewer, can find prints "suitable" for enlargement—suitable in the sense that they document or dramatize (preferably both) an event.†

From 1946—when Duncan joined the staff at *Life*—and through the early 1950s his contact sheets revealed action and violence. His first assignment took him to Iran, where he joined the spring migration of 200,000 Qashqai tribesmen in a parade of camels, donkeys, hunters and horsemen, women and children. His photos showed the sweep of the huge movement and the sturdy dignity in the faces of the Qashqai, who made the Missouri nomad an honorary *khan* in their tribe. Next, he went to Palestine, and his camera caught the turbulence of the Promised Land during the partition . . . Barbed wire, bombs, terrorism, the sad, suffering face of Dr. Chaim Weizmann, the alert, tough Haganah, British troops at bay . . . Jewish refugees on leaky, outmoded ships, peasants in the hills of Galilee. Death, explosions, blockades, gun battles—Dave Duncan covered Arabs and Jews impartially—and both sides shot at him with equal impartiality. He was the first correspondent to break the Arab ban on U. S. journalists during the Palestine crisis; and he photographed King Abdullah of Transjordan and King Ibn-Saud of Saudi Arabia when the ancient antagonists met to pledge a joint fight for Arab independence.

His Yankee hide still intact, Duncan moved on to the Turkish straits, to Bulgaria, next to India and the fratricidal fight between Moslems and Hindus; and then, Egypt (1947), Saudi Arabia, Turkey and Greece (1948), India (early in 1950) and finally, Japan. On June 25, 1950, he was relaxing in Tokyo, having just finished part one of a big photo essay on Japanese art. It was hot, sunny, and humid, and he had joined the mass exodus to the beach. Then came the terse news bulletin about Korea, and he sped back to MacArthur's headquarters, studied the reports, and by early Tuesday was winging toward the new war.

Korea was Duncan's great photographic triumph. It brought him

---

† Future historians ought to have access to the contact sheets of top news photographers, whose visual notes would provide a framework of authenticity to written history.

international acclaim; from it came *This Is War*, the brilliant book that propelled him to the front rank of war photographers alongside the likes of Mathew Brady and Robert Capa. He was thirty-four, a veteran of World War II; a photographer but also a Marine, he wore the emblem of the Corps on his old baseball cap and carried a pack on his back. He carried two 35 mm cameras slung like bandoliers across the chest of his field jacket. He was on the Suwon airfield when the ancient Syngman Rhee, President of South Korea, flew in with the American ambassador. He stood watching when a C-54 named *Bataan* landed a few minutes later, and Douglas MacArthur carrying his long-stemmed corncob pipe, alighted. He followed MacArthur north on the general's first tour of inspection. The road churned with refugees and truckloads of South Korean troops headed south, away from the front. He was discouraged by the chaos, but cheered by General MacArthur's composure. He wrote in *This Is War*:

> At the crossroads of Yongdunpo where the road branched, one fork turning east into Seoul, we could plainly see northern artillery fire landing upon the south bank of the river less than one mile away. Standing directly at the crossroads, MacArthur was given a hasty briefing on the terrain and known positions. The absolute arrogance and almost exasperating belligerence with which he stood in that intersection delighted me.

During the war's second week, American troops were sped from Japan to try to stem the flood of North Koreans storming down from the 38th parallel. Duncan watched the outnumbered 24th Division fight a stubborn, yard-by-yard delaying action to slow down the Communists. In that week, too, he became the first photographer ever to fly aboard an Air Force jet on a strafing and rocket mission. Late in July, 1950, he covered South Koreans as they fought on the slopes of Hill 626, whose top, held by Communists, was a vital position in the Pusan Perimeter. He was on hand to cover the United Nations' first large infantry attack led by U. S. Marines, who landed early in August. The First Marine Brigade had walked ashore safely at Pusan because the brave troops of the U. S.

Eighth Army under General Walton Walker had held the Perimeter although they were outmanned and outgunned. The Leathernecks, young and tough, many of them wearing the traditional service tattoos—"Death Before Dishonor," "Mother," "U. S. Marines"—were ready to fight. And Duncan was ready to document their heroism and suffering.

"Nearly every man in this book is a U. S. Marine," he wrote in the introduction to *This Is War*. "Having shared their lives, as they did mine, during three years while moving up out of the South Pacific islands and right into Tokyo Bay . . . I took it for granted, when they arrived in Korea, that I would photograph their battles." The book is dedicated to two Marines, a rifleman who was critically wounded and a machine-gunner who was killed in action. It is a "story" in three parts —*The Hill, The City, Retreat, Hell.*—each of which is preceded by blocks of text. There are no captions in the pictorial sections, which cover the Marines from the first week in September until Christmas, 1950. In them, Duncan used photos the way Hemingway used words in his fiction—to show "the way it was." As Duncan explained in his introduction, he "wanted to show what war did to a man"; to catch the camaraderie, the bravery, suffering, agony and confusion. "I wanted," he said, "to tell a story of war, as war has always been for men through the ages. Only their weapons, the terrain, the causes have changed."

To show all these things a photographer must get as close to battle— and death—as a combatman. He must feel what they are feeling when machine gun fire rakes a field or when enemy artillery zeros in. Not only did Duncan crawl alongside infantrymen, he got in front of them to photograph their charges. When they stormed a hill, he stormed with them. When they zigzagged through the streets to mop up the city of Seoul, he was at their sides. He shared their foxholes and their fears; he photographed the pain on their faces and the tears in their eyes.

When the First Marine Division was encircled in northeast Korea, Duncan somehow got into Kotori and joined his trapped buddies. Thus, he was the only photographer to record their withdrawal to the Japan Sea. In the wicked cold of December, 1950, he marched along with the frostbitten U. N. troops down the road called "Nightmare Alley." For members of the Corps it was a Dunkirk, and David Douglas Duncan, still a Marine at heart, shared their bitterness and agony.

Duncan's intense identification with the Marines, his willingness to share their ordeals and dangers, gave *This Is War* the impact of a powerful though wordless novel. Like a work of serious fiction, the book's "characterizations" were well-rounded and strong; the story was universal, true and meaningful. Published in 1951, *This Is War* was considered by Edward Steichen to be the greatest book of war photographs ever published. Its sharpness of focus and depth assure it a permanemt place in the library of books that bare the heart and soul of men at war.

After Korea, David Duncan continued his "normal" pursuit of images on a global scale—Germany, Egypt, Indochina, Afghanistan, the U. S. S. R., Ireland—and produced his superb picture books. In 1966, he was interviewed on a television show. Asked what he would do now that *Yankee Nomad* was finished, he replied that he didn't have the slightest notion what he would do or where he would go. He didn't even know where he was going after he left the TV studio. And that answer, of course, is the only answer a true vagabond can ever give.

Horst Faas of the Associated Press.

Horst Faas

A U. S. soldier leaps from a hovering helicopter into a deadly thicket of shattered and charred tree stumps in Vietnam, April, 1966. (AP photos by Horst Faas)

A Vietnamese litter bearer wears a mask to blot out the smell of death as he passes bodies of U. S. and Vietnamese soldiers slain by Viet Cong, November, 1965.

A mother weeps for her badly wounded daughter as Vietnamese troops pass by in pursuit of Viet Cong guerrillas, September, 1963.

The Battle of Dong Xoai: A Vietnamese Ranger sprints into action after jumping from a chopper.

5. The Cool War of Horst Faas

THE BATTLE of Dong Xoai started at night, but the photographer did not learn about it until the next morning. When news reached Saigon, Horst Faas quickly donned his combat clothes, collected his camera gear, and sped toward Bien Hoa, a military airport fifteen miles north of the city. Close to the field his vehicle had a flat tire, and while he was changing it the first wave of helicopters took off. Watching their departure, the photographer felt "miserable"; he knew that usually a correspondent had to ride the first wave of a relief operation, because that is when "things happen." As he sweated out the tire another wave of choppers headed toward the battle. At Dong Xoai, the first and second waves were wiped out by the Viet Cong, but the third group landed safely. And Horst Faas, a husky man with the shoulders of a lumberjack, jumped in with wave number three.

He landed on a soccer field that sunny afternoon in June, 1965. A storm of bullets greeted him, so he leaped into a ditch with the soldiers, and started to shoot pictures. Battle raged throughout the day and through the night as South Vietnamese Rangers fought to retake the little district town of Dong Xoai. The night before, 2,000 Viet Cong had overwhelmed the town's 400 militiamen, killing all but fifteen of the defenders. Now, the tough V. C. were defending their positions with great stubbornness, punishing the Rangers for every yard of ground they regained.

Darting along to record the action, Horst Faas was swept into a swirl of death and destruction. "Every ten seconds a man would fall," he said.

Once an American adviser, thinking they might be overrun, told him to grab a compass and be ready to strike out into the bush. Spotting a helicopter about to return to Saigon, the photographer considered climbing aboard. Luckily he did not, for the Communists riddled the craft with heavy fire, killing many of its occupants.

In the confusion of battle, everybody seemed to be running. Looking across a road, Faas noticed a "friendly" face popping in and out of a bunker fifteen feet away. He photographed the man, who looked bemused. A South Vietnamese soldier pointed at the bunker laughing and indicating: "V. C. V. C.!" A couple of minutes later a bomb hit the bunker and Faas knew that that V. C. must have been blown up.

By the time the Rangers drove off the V. C. the next day, Faas had a powerful collection of photos, which made the lead story in *Life* magazine, July 2, 1965. The photos caught the savage, nightmarish quality of the war: a wounded Seabee, face pained and shocked; a Ranger falling with bullets in his legs; a militiaman weeping at the news his family has been killed; soldiers under heavy fire; a little boy feeding his infant sister while the mother sits in stupor; a family crying with hysterical relief at being alive; a girl hobbling on a makeshift crutch toward a helicopter; a stream of refugees carrying their pitiful sticks of property away from the battlefield. These were the kind of photographs that made Horst Faas the top photographer of the Vietnam War, and the first cameraman ever to win the Pulitzer Prize and the Robert Capa Award in the same year, 1965. (The Robert Capa Award of the Overseas Press Club is given in memory of the great photographer who was killed in Indochina. The citation to Horst Faas reads, "for superlative photography requiring exceptional courage and enterprise in Vietnam.")

Horst Faas of the Associated Press has been in Vietnam since 1962, and twice, in '63 and '64, he was cited by the OPC for his outstanding photos. A courageous, daring man—one general called him "the luckiest man alive"—he is modest about his bravery. In *Popular Photography* (March, 1966), he was asked by writer Betty Brown if he "thinks of himself as brave":

"No. No, no, no. Nobody's brave. That's a bad word. You get used to it. You learn. You learn. That's the only way. When bravery begins, then stupidity begins too—especially in photography. When somebody thinks he has to take a picture, for *any* price, that's rather stupid. Going into Dong Xoai was a great thing, but I wouldn't do it again. Even for 15–20 pages in *Life,* I wouldn't do this again."

He never takes a stupid risk, and refuses to go into battle with inept troops. He checked the Vietnamese Rangers before going into Dong Xoai, and judged them fit to fight. "Even so," he said later, "I may have gone a little bit off my judgment on Dong Xoai. That was too much of a risk."

Know-how, judgment, coolness under fire—the qualities of the first-rate correspondent were acquired by Horst Faas in a life saturated with the sights and sounds of war. Born in Berlin, April 28, 1933, he is the oldest son of Adalbert and Gerda Faas. He has two brothers: Peter, an engineer, living in Regensburg; and Egbert, a teacher of languages at the University of Würzburg. His parents now live in Munich, where Adalbert Faas is the Bavarian representative of *Deutche Kaliverkaufsstelle,* Germany's largest producer and marketeer of chemical fertilizers.

Growing up in a nation committed to military conquest, young Horst recalls, "My schooltime was from beginning to end marked and often dominated by the events of the war and the bad years that followed the war." The family moved several times: from Berlin during intense Allied air raids; to Eastern Silesia when his father was transferred; from Eastern Silesia when the Russian Army advanced; from Berlin, again, in 1945 because conditions were unbearable; from Salzwedel (home of his grandparents) when the American Army handed it over to the Russians. Between 1945 and 1949, the Faas family moved several times within West Germany, finally settling in Munich, Bavaria.

The wandering years are hazy to Horst Faas, who does not remember the names of the schools he went to. "I changed schools about sixteen times between '41 and '48," he says. Yet he feels, curiously, that his childhood, as far as he can remember, "was just as one would imagine any other childhood. When I was eight years old we collected shrapnel from Allied bombing in the Berlin Grunewald as other kids today will collect champignons there (if the Grunewald still exists). When air raids sounded we ran home just like kids today run when it rains. But we did not run faster because of air raid alerts than we would because of rain."

Unlike an American youngster, he had no hobbies and played no competitive sports. But he liked skiing, swimming, mountain wandering and climbing. From his early days he developed an enthusiasm "for running through the woods and sleeping under the stars. My school went up in flames several times during the war and often I also could go skiing into the mountains because the schools had no heating."

It was a grim time to grow up—a time when a boy is robbed of childhood, when his character is forged in a rootless, violent environment. Yet there is neither self-pity nor bitterness in Horst Faas, merely an admirable, lucid honesty that concedes that "I might have grown up much faster than kids do today. At the end of the war I felt quite independent." And rightly so. He had helped his mother escape the Russians, to scrounge for food and transportation in an exploding landscape—and, finally, just to survive.

Those years made him, as he now says, "versatile and alert and able to adjust myself to ever-changing situations and impressions. They also taught me—from the age of ten on—that nothing brings so much success and recognition as hard work. The war, and especially the years after, also taught me that hardships are never as hard as they seem at the time they occur, and they can be endured."

He graduated from high school in the spring of 1951, and searched for a job in the newspaper business in Munich. He landed one with Keystone, a British newsphoto agency, at $15.00 a month, starting in the darkroom and moving to clerical work and then to an apprenticeship on the night desk. Meanwhile, he was studying economics and sociology at the University of Munich. In 1952, he worked in Berlin and Frankfurt and studied at the universities of both cities, but after the Berlin revolution of 1953 he gave up formal study. From then on he got his journalistic education on the job. When a photographer in Frankfurt was too hungover to cover an assignment, he took his first photograph. The subject was Chancellor Adenauer, who was visiting a flower show in Wiesbaden. Faas took a camera and flash gun and, experimenting, made four exposures of Dr. Adenauer smelling a rose.

In 1956, the Associated Press hired Horst Faas as a news photographer, because he knew how to get a picture. Far from a polished cameraman, he used his wits to conceal a lack of skill. The first day he worked in Frankfurt a building collapsed and buried fifty people. The AP office handed him a Speed Graphic camera, which he knew nothing about. On the spot, he asked a UPI cameraman how to handle the camera, how to load it and trigger the shutter. He took his picture and rushed it to the office and beat the competition. His employers thought he was an experienced big-camera photographer—and he never told them otherwise until much later.

From 1956 to 1960 he worked out of the Bonn bureau, covering mainly West German politics. Then he went to the Congo, where, in September, 1961, he was beaten by Katangan troops and forced to eat his United Nations pass. However, his photographs were drawing respect from editors around the world. His next stop was Algeria, and after that country became independent Horst Faas went to Vietnam.

He took with him ingenuity, energy, intelligence—and a special kind of experience which gave him an edge on his competitors. In January, 1967, in a letter from Saigon, he told the author:

"The experience of the big war as a child and of the bad times after the war as a teenager and the experience of a number of 'little' wars—I think have given me some advantages over reporters that see their first person shot dead in a war. The benefits of experience? A more balanced view of the brutal events of wartimes, a less emotional approach to stories, a good eye for the exceptional scene in the big war theatre. And a good sense for the real drama (which is the best news story and gives the best pictures in war) that develops between humans every day, and is so difficult for newcomers, to be found in the giant machinery of war."

For a correspondent, war is an obstacle course, with tricky, difficult and sometimes dangerous hurdles to leap:

"The main problem," Faas says, "as always in reporting with the camera is to be at the right place at the right time—and then get the stuff out as fast and as good as possible. Wars seem always to be fought in places where communications for radiophotos are lousy. Vietnam is no better than the Congo, where the big problem was communications and transportation—no planes, no cars, no permits, no authorities that would help us. Transportation in Vietnam is comparatively easy. Military planes take the reporter everywhere. . . .

"In Algeria a photographer had to overcome total censorship, possible assassination—a popular way to get rid of reporters—and again transportation. . . . In Laos transportation and absolutely wrong reports from every faction. Most of the battles we rushed to cover and which were reported never happened. In New Guinea it was the complete dependence on the Dutch military—without them no food, housing, communication, transport. . . . In Vietnam so many units are fighting in so many places in such a vast country that it is very difficult to hit the right places at the right time."

The war in Vietnam is vertical, a leapfrog war that moves from airfield to airfield, from unit to unit. A correspondent has to be patient, persistent, energetic and tough. Faas says:

"Hard continuous work and constant trying are the only way to hit the jackpot occasionally. Good judgment as to which operations will be photo productive, which will be good news stories, helps a lot. Since fights usually are very short for the little group the photographer is with, it also is imperative that he does not lose his head. He must avoid panic and use every chance to get pictures. It doesn't pay to go on an operation if you're not willing to risk a bit for pictures. It's the five minutes *guts* and not the five days walking that gets the pictures."

Because of the nature of war in Vietnam, Faas has seen more fire-fights than most GIs.

"There is more small unit coverage in this war than in any other war," he explains. "Even the 'big battles' are an accumulation of many small fights, and that's why we have to go with the little 30-man platoon to get the action we want to record. World War II and Korea saw most reporters at a division level; it was always possible to get up front somehow by jeep. In Vietnam most real reporters work on a platoon level."

When Faas is not in the field, he works as a photographer and photo editor in Saigon. Since he is a skillful all-around journalist, he writes news stories, edits copy, and captions pictures. He dispatches the stuff by radio and air freight. In his "spare moments" he checks government and military news sources by telephone. It is a full schedule, from 7:30 A. M. to 11:00 P. M., Monday through Sunday.

When word of action flashes into Saigon—a battle such as Dong Xoai—Horst Faas climbs into his field uniform. He carries a pack with a two-day supply of food, a tent, air mattress, blanket—and a waterproof camera case. "Once with the unit," he says, "I try to get a briefing, looking for the platoon or company which is likely to see action or is already most heavily engaged."

His understanding of soldiering is comprehensive. He knows how to size up a situation, how to win the confidence of GIs and Vietnamese, when to move up—or out—and where to be when the bullets start flying. To get immediate news during an engagement, he sticks close to a radio—but not directly behind it, because the radioman is a magnet for snipers. When a fire-fight starts, he stays low, never joining clusters of soldiers (they are grenade targets), but never straying from the main group. At night, he looks for a hole or digs a deep one, close to the command post. Since picture-taking is out of the question, he spends the evening talking to GIs about the daily operation. To get a good night's sleep, he uses soundproof earplugs that are capable of blocking out artillery fire.

Through experience and careful thought, this superb photographer has worked out a personal code to guide him in his relationship with combatmen. Although the ground rules vary with the kind of troops— American, Vietnamese, Australian—paratroopers, Rangers, Marines— officers, sergeants, buck privates—pilots and foot soldiers—the following code applies everywhere:

*Never tell anybody his business. A green, shaky officer should not be told how to line up his troops.

*Don't try to be different, pointing out that you are a civilian. Soldiers don't like this.

*Share the hardships and dangers of the men. Sleep on the ground for a few nights, just as they do. The best stories and picture situations develop when soldiers and commanders find out you are one of them. That you are NOT coming in for a few minutes to see them burning down houses, getting shot and wounded. Soldiers who don't trust you don't talk to you—and don't like you around when things get dangerous.

*Be considerate. Don't get in the way when things get rough. A photographer should not be a burden to troops. Everyone in the field should have his military gear—and camping equipment. I try not to give any commander, squad or battalion level, the feeling he must protect and care for me on an operation.

*The war photographer has not the right but the privilege to see intimate things such as death and wounds, swears and prayers. I make it a policy NOT to photograph people that are awaiting evacuation for hospitals long after they were wounded, and NOT to photograph wounded in hospitals or tents. Up front, where soldiers get wounded, usually nobody minds when a camera records the action.

*Be critical of what anybody may tell you. A nineteen-year old may tell war stories that sound like the battle of Stalingrad all over. A battalion commander may have only brief and dry information about a dramatic event.

*Showing friendliness and consideration on every level is the best way to get the job done. This doesn't mean that you should be buddy-buddy.

*Overlook—and don't photograph—the little things that happen and are not supposed to happen. When one GI—against orders—slaps a prisoner, that should not go into every newspaper from New York to Hanoi. It is not typical, not news. If a Marine battalion burns a village under orders, that should be photographed and published. Most combat soldiers support this attitude; and if they know that a photographer can distinguish between the typical and the accidental—he will be welcomed again and get all the support he needs for a story.

*I do not carry weapons, but otherwise dress like a soldier, including steel helmet. Without a weapon a correspondent is not mistaken for a frustrated civilian adventurer, who goes out for kicks and shooting rather than as a professional reporter. I have never needed a weapon to defend myself. I don't think it makes sense to run around with a loaded pistol.

The code of Horst Faas is a model of objectivity and good sense. He is in Vietnam to do an honest, skillful job of reportage. "Besides this," he says, "my obligation is to give the day-to-day news in photos that are comprehensive, descriptive and interpretive. When I take the camera to photograph an event, I like to compare myself to a good newswriter."

The honesty and clarity of Horst Faas give his work the authenticity of truth, simply recorded. He knows he is doing important work, but there is no self-importance in his make-up. His attitude comes through in his answers to these questions: Do you think your photographs have had a value other than documentation? Will they, in an educational sense, help make future wars less likely?

"I think that good photographs from Vietnam write the history of this war and all the events related to it as other photos wrote history since photographers accompanied combatants. Photography has been an equal addition to the written word since its invention. The Vietnam war—as far as photographic reporting is concerned—is an extremely well-covered war. This is not only due to the photographers but also to the fact that there has been no censorship of photos.

"I do not think that my photographs will make future wars less likely. But I think that they so far have been and will continue to be a contribution that serves the truth about what happened and how it happened. Readers and editors who have followed my work over the years tell me that they trust my reporting. This is a great compliment. Now, they read my stories and look at my pictures to find some clear water in the muddy mess of the Vietnam situation."

You can trust the photographs of Horst Faas, and that is a tribute to his talent and integrity—and a comfort to newspaper readers trying to understand the chaotic events. A cool and dedicated craftsman, he is carrying on in the tradition of Brady, Capa, Duncan and other great photographers at war.

SECTION III
TRIO

THEY MET in Paris, this talented trio: a Frenchman from Normandy, a Pole from Warsaw, and a Hungarian from Budapest. Their names were Henri Cartier-Bresson, David Seymour and Robert Capa. The time was the 1930s, when France shivered with unrest and Europe was poised on the precipice of violence. Capa and "Chim" and Cartier—citizens of the world, wanderers who would capture renown—were young men then. Their lives would cross and re-cross in the next two decades, like literary characters with "star-crossed" destinies.

Their stories are microcosms of those years when a continent was blown apart, when lives were uprooted, families destroyed, identities submerged and nations decimated in that dark struggle, World War II. They used their cameras like painters use sketchbooks, to capture quickly those elusive moments of truth that reveal the heart of human conflict. Their stories dramatize how men of artistry, with different backgrounds and points of view, sharing the universal virtues of integrity and conscience, are drawn to one another, and in the process the lives and work of each are fortified.

David "Chim" Seymour.

David Seymour

Two little girls with a doll, typical of the children Chim Seymour photographed for UNESCO after World War II. (Photos by David Seymour, Magnum)

After World War II, children played in the ruins and rubble.

When asked to draw a picture, this Polish girl was so disturbed by her experience during the war that she could produce only a scrawl on the blackboard.

The faces of boys such as these, orphaned by war, captivated Chim Seymour.

1. The Children of Chim

HE WAS a sensitive, reserved man with a large forehead and the benevolent face of a miniature Buddha. He was a musician and a linguist; a superb chess player and a connoisseur of food and wine, of art and literature. His mind was both deep and broad; he was aware. Not only did he understand politics and society; he understood his own thinking about them. A cosmopolitan, a friend of the famous—Arturo Toscanini, Alberto Moravia, Ingrid Bergman—he knew a score of celebrities. Cautious, rather passive, he wasn't the type you'd expect to see in a hurly-burly profession. He died a violent death, the result of a single capricious act. But before he died this gentle man took a gallery of photographs that dramatizes how war devastates children.

His name was David Szymin; he changed it to David Seymour. But to the world of photography he will always be known as "Chim," the credit line he used for years. Although he photographed a wide variety of subjects—glamorous women, the grandeurs of the Vatican, great museums—his most poignant pictures were of the wandering children of postwar Europe—pained and homeless, their eyes shadowed with sadness and their bodies twisted from hunger . . . A little girl hugging a broken doll, an orphan boy weeping on the shoulder of a stranger, an urchin pleading for food . . . From infants to young adults—in France, Greece, Poland, Hungary, Czechoslovakia, Austria and Germany—thirteen million abandoned children roamed the Continent. Their photographer was Chim, the compassionate, the photographer of displaced persons, because he was one of them.

He was born on November 20, 1911, in Warsaw, Poland. His father, Benjamin Szymin, was a pioneer publisher of Hebrew and Yiddish authors such as Sholem Asch. A witty, lively man, Benjamin Szymin loved to dance and have a good time. His mother was sensitive and intelligent, interested in the fine arts. It was a solid middle-class family, happy and secure—until 1914. Then Chim, only three years old, experienced war for the first time. The German Army had invaded Poland, and the Szymins fled to the Ukraine to live with relatives. They moved from the small town of Orsha to Minsk, and then to Odessa in 1916, where they settled until their repatriation in 1919. Chim's older sister, Mrs. Eileen Shneiderman, of New York, the only member of the family alive, remembers the experience quite well:

"The first winter in Russia was hard and David caught rheumatism, which he suffered from all his life. His legs were very weak."

War and wandering—this was to be the destiny of David "Chim" Seymour. At eight years of age he already spoke a second language, Russian, and would become fluent in six others. A gifted child, he started to read very early, and by the time he was eight was reading such Russian classics as Tolstoy and Dostoevsky. He began to study the piano when he was ten.

"He was a bookish boy," his sister recalls, "quiet and bright. Shy and introspective. When he was about sixteen years of age, he changed. I had been studying journalism in Berlin and when I returned, I hardly recognized him. He had become very sociable—girls and parties and many friends. Such a change! He even acted like a father toward younger children."

After graduating from high school he was uncertain about his future. He had given up the idea of a career as a classical musician when he discovered he did not have perfect pitch. His father wanted him in the family business and sent the boy to Leipzig Academy to study graphic arts. Germany was then the world center of the new profession of photojournalism, the fatherland of such brilliant cameramen as Dr. Erich Salomon and Alfred Eisenstaedt. Photography had been a hobby with Chim, and now he took it up seriously while studying at the Academy.

In 1931, he returned to Poland, where his father's business was declining. There was no work for Chim, and after a six months' visit, he left home again. A wave of anti-Semitism—an evil omen for Europe—was sweeping Poland. This, and the lack of opportunity, drove Chim to Paris. He would study at the Sorbonne and polish his métier; he would become friends for life with photographers Robert Capa and Henri Cartier-Bresson. But David Seymour would never have a real home again.

Paris, 1931, still had the gaiety and playfulness of the roaring 1920's. The great depression—the "Wall Street Crack," the French called it—wouldn't reach France until 1932. So Paris was a romantic place for a young man trying to make his way in life. The gifted Chim searched for assignments. Breaking into photojournalism is difficult at any time, and it was doubly so in the early 1930s. There were not nearly so many magazines stressing photography then; *Life* and *Look* had not been born yet. Readers were not as attuned to reportorial photography as they are today. The competition for jobs was stiff, and with countless gifted people pouring into the good gray city—refugees from Europe and Asia—who knows how many talents withered without blooming? Chim was one of the resourceful ones who survived, for he had the will to achieve.

He had ideas, and ideas are as important as talent in the marketplace. And he associated with intellectuals—artists, writers, journalists—and the association helped him grow. He began to take reportorial pictures in and around Paris. He met Cartier-Bresson and Capa, and the three men shared a fifth-story walk-up "studio" and developed film in a closet. Their friendship was perhaps the most significant of his life. It refined his talent and eventually led to the formation of the Magnum Photo Agency, which would become his substitute "family" in later years.

Of the two men, the dynamic Robert Capa exerted the strongest influence on Chim. Their personalities were pitched to different keys: Capa dramatic and daring, challenged the world; Chim, predictable and prudent, underplayed his role. Chim admired the ingenious Hungarian, whose achievements were to become a constant challenge. The paths of the two men would crisscross often in the years to come; they and

Cartier-Bresson would meet in New York and Paris and elsewhere in affectionate reunions. A pivotal experience for all three was the Spanish Civil War, crackling across the nearby frontier.

Chim's Spanish photographs showed the impact of war on noncombatants—men, women and children. His photo essay of Barcelona illustrated what happens to a city when bombs rain upon it. Looking at these pictures, you can feel the terror of people who must live like moles to stay alive. When the Loyalist government collapsed, Chim returned to Paris, where he received an invitation from the Mexican government to cover the voyage of the S. S. *Sinai*. The ship carried over a thousand Spanish war refugees, to whom Mexico had offered asylum.

On the move again, Chim photographed the flights of the refugees. He spent several months in Mexico, moving on to New York, where there was to be an exhibition of his photographs at the Mexican embassy. Another country, new customs, another language—Chim added English to his portfolio, and changed his name to Seymour. When World War II broke out he was working in a darkroom. Despite poor eyesight he joined the U. S. Air Force, was assigned to a language school at Camp Ritchie, and shipped overseas to the European Theater of Operations. His photographic training and European background made him valuable; he worked in the photo reconnaissance and interpretation section of Air Force intelligence. Wearing thick horn-rimmed glasses under a pulled-down cap, Chim was a comical "swashbuckler." But his intellect and experience were formidable as he briefed high-ranking officers of SHAEF, and by war's end he would earn a commission as a lieutenant and become a U. S. citizen.

In September, 1944, he was in Paris, just a few days after the Germans pulled out. At a café in the Boulevard Montparnasse he ran into an old friend, John Morris. By the wildest chance, Morris was about to go to a party. Would Chim like to go? He would indeed! It was an amazing coincidence, for Cartier-Bresson and Bob Capa were there and the trio held a rousing reunion.

After the war, Chim stayed in Europe, like so many American GIs. But unlike most, his mission was a sad one; he searched the wreckage of the Continent for pieces of the past—for friends and family. His mother and father were dead, murdered by the Nazis in 1942 in the ghetto of Otwock, near Warsaw. He learned this while on assignment for UNESCO. He was taking pictures for a booklet, "Children of Europe," and a visit to Warsaw confirmed the fate of his parents. The shock must have been sickening; it shows in the tormented faces of Chim's "Children," the uprooted victims of war. Tragic, tender photographs, they evoked immediate sympathy.

Life remade its Christmas issue (1948) to give special position to this powerful photo essay. It was his greatest story, the one his friends point to when the name David "Chim" Seymour comes up. These pictures—some appear in this chapter—were picked for a posthumous exhibition of his work at the Art Institute of Chicago, in the spring of 1957. At the time, Peter Pollack, Curator of Photography, wrote:

"To Chim, wars—all wars—became an enormous crime against children. His photographs are monuments of this stark truth, a warning, a permanent cry to remember forever that all children are one the world over."

The thoughtful, reserved little bachelor loved toy stores. When he was in New York he always went to F. A. O. Schwarz and bought toys for his niece and nephew or the children of friends such as photographer Elliot Erwitt, Bill Downs of CBS, and Ingrid Bergman. He regarded every special occasion—an anniversary, a birthday—as an opportunity to play Santa Claus, to assemble toys and play with children. They found him amusing; his odd, wispy appearance appealed to their sense of joy and humor. And for him—timid of marriage—they represented the family he would never have.

For the last ten years of his life he lived in Europe, mainly in Paris and Rome. His assignments took him north to Scandinavia and south to the Mediterranean—to Greece, North Africa, and to the pioneer state of Israel, whose heroic efforts he so admired. Rome fascinated him, too; he was an expert on the Vatican and made memorable pictures of Pius XII and Cardinal Montini, who later became Pope Paul VI. He was an antiquarian who loved to prowl remote places. In 1954, upon the death of his good friend Robert Capa, he became president of Magnum Photos, and was a skillful administrator who brought "clarity"—his favorite word—to the agency. He had an apartment in Rome and was working on two books. The vagabondage of the photojournalist was beginning to pall ("I'm settling down, you see," he told his sister).

When war struck Suez in 1956, he was shooting pre-Olympic pictures in Greece and searching for antiquities in spare moments. He joined other journalists in Athens as they chartered a plane to take them to Cyprus. One of the correspondents, Frank White of Time-Life, wrote of Chim's last days, in a published letter.

> We stayed at the Ledra Palace Hotel at Nicosia. The place was a madhouse of frustrated correspondents. Characteristically, David was cool and reserved, spent his time studying dispatches, evaluating what was going on elsewhere, appraising events. . . . Before dawn Monday morning, he covered the take-off of French paratroop forces and later that day the return of the transport pilots. On Tuesday, *Newsweek*'s Ben Bradlee, David and myself negotiated ourselves a flight to Port Said on French Admiral Barjot's plane. Our accreditation with the French forces came through that night and we left by plane for Port Said early Wednesday morning. . . .
>
> Almost immediately, Bradlee, Dave and I picked up on *Match*'s Jean Roy [a photographer for *Paris Match* magazine]. He'd liberated two jeeps and a truck, procured gas by signing chits over the name, "Petain, marechal de France." . . . For the next forty hours or so, Roy drove us through the streets of Port Said. There were dead bodies, food riots, some sniping, prowling Allied tanks, patrols and a seething mass of hostile Egyptians.
>
> Dave must have known what he was letting himself in for. Ben Bradlee and I made no secret of the fact that we were scared to death. But Dave, the quiet rational man, the intellectual . . . said nothing. He just kept on making pictures. . . .
>
> When making pictures, he seemed to be an entirely different man. He kept saying, "This is a great story." I got the impression that he felt this made him somehow impervious to risk.

White and Bradlee left for Cyprus that Thursday in November to file their stories. Jean Roy and Chim stayed on. On November 10, 1956, four days after the armistice, they went in a jeep to photograph an exchange of wounded at El Qantara. It should have been a routine job; the truce had been declared. But something strange happened. The photographers zoomed through the Anglo-French lines and drove down the causeway toward the Egyptians about 600 yards away. A jittery Egyptian opened fire with a machine gun, and the riddled jeep plunged into the Sweetwater Canal, killing both men.

The death of Chim—the peaceful man—was ironic and out of character. He was no soldier of fortune; even his decision to go to Europe was surprising, though perhaps, as president of Magnum, he felt obligated to do so. Although his death was violent and unnecessary, his life was fulfilled. He left a legacy of tenderness and compassion. One of his last photographs, taken the day before he was shot, shows a man, woman and child. On the shoulders of the grizzled Egyptian is a barefoot little girl, her face solemn, her eyes looking straight ahead as though searching for the future.

Henri Cartier-Bresson.

Henri Cartier-Bresson

2. The Elusive Cartier-Bresson

THE CHANCES are you have never seen his face, although he is famous. He prefers anonymity, to move unobtrusively and freely among people. He moves quickly and quietly and hardly ever is seen without a 35 mm camera in his hands or dangling from his wrist. His reflexes are as sharp as those of a great athlete—a Mickey Mantle, a Jimmy Brown or an Arnold Palmer. His powers of concentration are fierce. He has a dry wit and delights in ducking pointed questions. Once,

The Kashmir Pass, 1948: A rest amid the beauty of the mountains. (Photos by Henri Cartier-Bresson, Magnum)

while taking pictures at the Parke-Bernet Galleries in New York City, he was approached by a lady with a question.

"Are you from the press?" she asked.

He felt that it was impolite to answer with a simple yes or no. Instead he replied: "I'm just a maniac." Whereupon the lady answered:

"Oh, that's perfectly all right."

The truth of the man's droll answer is that he *does* have a mania—a mania for photography. Henri Cartier-Bresson is subtle, gifted, blessed with iron integrity; he is an artist who uses photography "as a means of drawing, instantaneously, intuitively with a mechanical instrument."

Cartier-Bresson was born on August 22, 1908, in the small village of Chanteloup. He belongs to a family of thread manufacturers. Henri's younger brother is in the cotton business and his sister became a poet. Cartier was reared in Paris and attended the Fenelon school and the Lycée Condorcet. At the age of twenty, he decided to study painting in

Dessau, Germany, 1945: In a camp of displaced persons, a Gestapo informer—pretending to be a refugee—is exposed by an enraged woman.

André Lhote's studio. In 1931 he bought a Leica camera in Marseilles—and soon after, photography became his life. While maintaining a deep preoccupation with painting, Cartier realized the impossibility of doing two things at the same time with integrity.

He was to travel around the world, from the villages of Africa, India and China, to the great cities of Asia, Europe and the Americas. His artist's eye and diamond-sharp mind made him the master of a modern form of photography, an instantaneous and spontaneous form. He wanders from place to place, searching for what he calls "decisive moments"—moments of great beauty or tragedy, moments of historical significance. The moment must be caught immediately, before it vanishes forever, so Cartier composes his picture instantly—and snaps the shutter. He has captured hundreds of these moments; his photographs have been published in dozens of magazines; his work has been exhibited numerous times. His books include: *The Photographs of Henri Cartier-Bresson; From One China to Another; China; Danses à Bali; The Europeans;* and *The Decisive Moment.* He is one of the great photographers of the twentieth century.

His close friends and associates call him "Hank Carter" and they marvel at his photographic discipline and at the meticulousness of his imagery. He is not easy to know, but he is a delight to interview. Courteous and articulate, he talked with me in an office high above the streets of Manhattan. In a quiet, clear voice he answered questions with great precision, recording his feelings about war in a long, taped interview.

The midmorning sun outlined his sensitive face; his blue eyes were brilliant and intense behind his glasses. Occasionally he shifted restlessly in his chair, tapping on the desk with a slender hand. There was tension in him—the tension of great energy carefully controlled—and you would not have been surprised if he had bounded up, like a cat in flight.

"In my time," Cartier said, "we've been involved with many social problems and political problems, some of which turned into war. The Spanish Civil War marked my generation very much. It was my first experience at seeing people dying. I hardly took any photographs in Spain. But I had been doing documentary film on medical help to Republican Spain. Then I was drafted, in World War II, into a film and photo unit of the French Army. At the collapse of France I was captured and was a prisoner of war in Germany for three years."

His second taste of war, his life as a prisoner of war, had a profound impact on Cartier-Bresson. His eyes narrowed as he spoke of it:

"When I was captured I had hidden my camera at a nearby farm. So all of the pictures I would have taken just remained in my eyes. All that I have seen and couldn't photograph has marked me for the rest of my life. There are things I can't forget; I can forgive but I can't forget. This has marked me very much, and I think it has marked anybody with consciousness."

Denied the camera, the tool of his profession, he was compelled to store up all those experiences and feelings which otherwise would have been translated into photographic images. But he feels that this was a valuable, albeit shattering, experience; it gave a new dimension to his life and work. It helped shape his point of view, without which no communicator can make a valid comment on the world about him. The first thing we all have to be is human, he insists, and the important thing is to know what we feel.

Like many other prisoners, Cartier-Bresson tried to escape from the Germans, failing in two attempts and being sent to worse camps after recapture. He talked about fear and about how it can be overcome through action and commitment to a purpose. He spoke of this with shyness, apologetic about being so personal:

"I remember the last time I had decided to escape. All night I was shivering, trembling and extremely nervous. Next morning when I woke up and it was really dangerous—being shot at by the sentry, taking risks— I was extremely calm because I had something to do. It's a little like seasickness. If you're a passenger and you have a weak stomach, you'll be sick. Whereas if you have something to do, if you're part of the crew, you don't feel the seasickness."

Periodically throughout the interview Cartier-Bresson asked to have the tape played back to make sure he had expressed himself with absolute clarity. It was a pleasant morning, and over the whir of the recorder the sounds of New York traffic drifted through the open window.

"After I escaped, I recovered my Leica and returned to France, where I worked in the Underground. Before the liberation I tried to organize press photographers into units to cover the departure of the Germans and the liberation of Paris. After the liberation I became a war correspondent in the French Army. Later I did a film on the homecoming of war prisoners and displaced persons for the American Office of War Information and for the French Ministry of war prisoners and displaced persons."

In 1947, Henri Cartier-Bresson went to the Far East and covered the war in Kashmir on both sides. In December, 1948, he flew from Rangoon to China, arriving in Peking twelve days before it was taken by Mao Tse-tung's troops. He left the capital by the last airplane before the Communists took the city. From Shanghai he searched for ways to get into the zones controlled by the Communists, finally crossing near Tsing-tao (in the Shantung Peninsula). There he encountered a journalist and businessman, and the three men decided to drive by jeep to the Communist lines.

On the last lap, Cartier, leading the way, walked toward the lines waving a white handkerchief and his passport.

The eerie whiteness of the snow and the sense of danger—the troops viewed them as suspicious interlopers—made the walk a nervous one. But the soldiers accepted them, and the photographer spent five weeks confined on a village farm and then returned to Shanghai. From there Cartier journeyed to Nanking, where he observed the departure of the last followers of Chiang Kai-shek and the arrival of the Communists. Late in September, 1949, he left China for India, to accompany the Indian Army in the "police action" against the Hyderabad state (where he had previously been with the private army, "the Rasahars").

The Spanish Civil War, World War II, the fighting in the Far East, the civil strife in China—these were his active participations in war.

"But throughout all our lives," Cartier said, "we photographers have had a preoccupation with war. Even when we weren't there, when we were sitting in Paris or New York, the presence of war in some part of the world affected us. Sometimes we couldn't cover it because we were busy on other projects. But the very idea that war was going on affected everybody."

In this pervading climate of war, the photographer confronts the same problems as the rest of us, but because he is also a commentator his dilemmas are sharper. What are his obligations to his profession, to humanity in general, to his country? To whom or to what is he responsible? What is his attitude?

"There are different kinds of war, of course," Cartier said, "and I feel the differentiations. A war for liberation is something you must participate in. It is for the betterment of humanity and you have to fight it, just as we fought World War II. The photographer cannot be a disinterested observer. He participates in what is going on in life; he is implicated. All of us are part of something larger than ourselves and must participate in some wars no matter what disgust we feel. But to fight a colonial war, a war of oppression, is shameful and atrocious. War does not solve any problems, it is a sign of weakness."

Suddenly he tilted his head a little; his eyes blinked, as though a series of images were racing through his head:

"The pictures of a photographer should be a comment. To make a comment you must know where you stand in relation to other human beings. You must have a set of references, a humanism."

Those who are communicators or commentators have a special obligation to be honest. The modern photographer is the spiritual descendant of not only Mathew Brady, but of artists such as Jacques Callot and Goya, whose legacy is truth. "Photography in Japanese is called 'Sha-Shing,' " Cartier pointed out. "It means 'copy-truth.' "

"The attitude today is the same as it was centuries ago," he went on. "You take the etchings of Callot in the seventeenth century during those terrible fights against the Protestants in the south of France. Or take Goya in the 'Disasters of War' [sketches and paintings of Spain's struggle against Napoleon]. Or take the photography of Brady or Capa, or that of Dave Duncan or Gene Smith and Carl Mydans and many, many others. All these men expressed the same human attitude, the same intellectual protest."

Cartier-Bresson does not "protest" in the way that Duncan or Capa or any "combat" photographer does. His greatest work has been done outside the battlefields, in the larger arena, where he has striven "to show the greatness of man facing his fate." His significance lies in his almost shivery awareness of the pervading atmosphere of war, and in his insight

142

into how it affects all of us. For this awareness is a reflection of how war has helped shape the point of view of a great photographer.

It is impossible to pin down exactly the nature of this influence. The human character is a mosaic, and the finer the person the finer the strands woven into him. Cartier-Bresson is a richly complex human being, impossible to unravel. His elusiveness and passion for anonymity serve practical purposes—enabling him to work with freedom—and also reveal how he looks at life. Commenting on anonymity, he said:

"I think it's a little like the sculptor who worked on medieval cathedrals. He wasn't concerned if his sculpture was on the top of a gate or a cathedral, at a main entrance or if it was on the top of a tower. He did it for the glory of God. We have to work for a concept and not for *me* or *I*."

His concept of picture-taking is almost priestly in its purity. Very few photographers are as dedicated to making the *next* picture as Cartier; for him the world is a perpetual diary and each photograph merely another page.

"We must pick the significant thing in the mass of flowing incidents," he said. "That where the decision is important to a photographer. He's going to be aiming at such a subject, how close must he be and from where and how visually can he express himself. All his being, his imagination, his whole culture, his human attitude—everything is implicated and that's what's interesting in photography."

After the interview, we walked across Manhattan, and though Henri Cartier-Bresson talked with precision, he seemed completely attuned to the visual world about him. He was carrying a 35 mm camera and, suddenly, like a cat after a mouse, he loped away and was taking pictures of a sailor and a girl in a doorway. One, two, three exposures—and he was back by my side, chatting quietly. The young couple hadn't noticed the photographer. Discreet, unobtrusive, anonymous: Cartier-Bresson.

Robert Capa.

Robert Capa

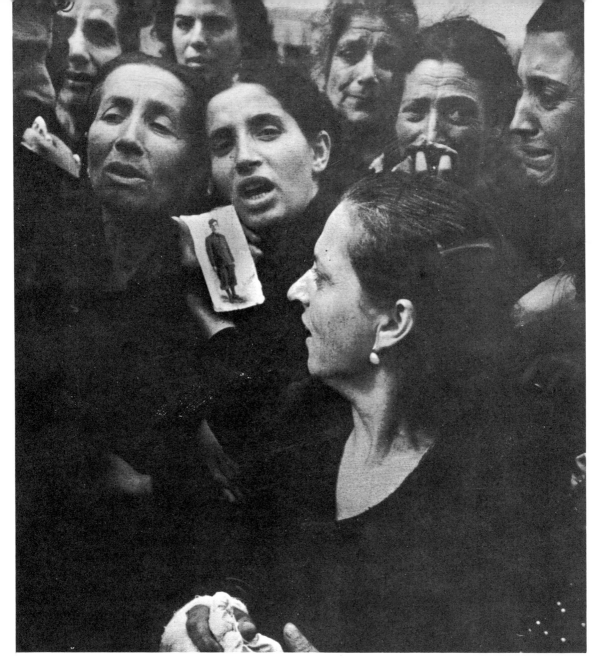

Italy, 1943: The mothers of Naples mourn the death of a son. (All photos by Robert Capa, Images of War, *copyright 1964)*

Indochina, 1954: Vietnamese widows with their children grieving at the graves of their fallen husbands was one of the last photos taken by Bob Capa.

This memorable World War II photo captures a soldier in the surf at Normandy.

3. Death Comes to Capa

"What are you doing here? Who called you here?"
—ERIC JENS PETERSEN

THE PHOTOGRAPHER sat in the front of the jeep, two cameras around his neck, a thermos of iced tea and a flask of cognac at his side. The mechanized column had been starting and stopping since early morning, pushing cautiously through sporadic gunfire and exploding land mines. Machines and men churned the earth to dust that rose and powdered the fields that flanked the roads.

The column stopped and Robert Capa jumped from the jeep. He had been in and out of the vehicle all day, photographing the French as they searched in the fields for enemy snipers. The war in Indochina was his fifth in eighteen years. He was not eager to go anymore; he had missed the Korean War deliberately. A few years before, he had said, "I am delighted to be an unemployed war correspondent. I hope to stay unemployed as a war photographer till the end of my life." However, when *Life* magazine approached him in Japan, requesting that he replace a photographer who had been called home, he agreed to make one more trip to the front.

On May 25, 1954, four weeks after flying into Hanoi, Robert Capa and two other journalists had ridden a jeep out of the city at 7:00 A. M., heading south to cover action in the Red River Delta. He was working on a photo essay based on the idea of contrasts—the deadly, mechanical impersonality of war set against the eternally hopeful peasants working in the fields. The Red River country was a natural setting for his theme, being one of the richest rice-producing areas in the world. The people still followed their old ways, plowing their paddies behind water buffalo.

By 2:15 of that sunny May afternoon the French forces, numbering about two thousand, halted under attack near Thai Binh, about forty-five miles southeast of Hanoi. As Capa got out of the jeep he spoke to his companions: "I'm going up the road; look for me when you drive up." With these words the handsome man with the roguish eyes walked off. At age forty-one, still quick and graceful, he was ready, as always, to move ahead of the troops to get a telling photograph.

Fifty-five minutes later Robert Capa lay dead in a small field. He had taken one stride too far and triggered a land mine. He had been in Spain to record the Civil War, in the Far East to witness one of the hottest battles between the Chinese and Japanese; he had followed World War II from the Battle of Britain to Berlin, and in 1948 had covered the fighting in Israel. After many dangerous years, death came to Capa in Indochina; and it came, as death often does, as a surprise—and from underfoot.

He was the epitome of gallantry, and his photographs symbolize our violent times. They show the degradation of war: men suffering and dying; women and children sorrowful and desolate; towns blasted to pieces by high explosives. And sometimes, too, his pictures show flashes of joy on the faces of people caught between scenes of death and destruction. If you look very closely at Capa's photographs, you will see the man who made them: a serious man, a man of integrity and compassion; strong and brave but tenderhearted. But all his adult life he would cover this seriousness with a veneer of wit and gaiety, giving the appearance of a classic *bon vivant*.

He called himself Capa but he was born André Friedmann, of middle-class parents, in Budapest in 1913. "I was born deeply covered by Jewish grandfathers on every side," he wrote in his book *"Slightly Out of Focus."* Those were chaotic days. South of his homeland two short wars (1912–1913) were fought in the Balkans and, instead of settling anything, merely prepared the way for World War I. Countries lost not only battles but their national identities; boundaries dissolved; Austria-Hungary split and became two nations. Old states such as Montenegro disappeared; new ones such as Albania and Czechoslovakia sprang up.

The face of Europe was changing and would change more during his lifetime.

Young André was a good student, but rather carefree about studying. As part of his classical education he studied Greek, beginning with the fifth grade in school. His flair for languages (he learned to speak five) later became the focus for many jokes, which greatly pleased him— pleased him so much that he cultivated a certain Hungarian quaintness in his speech. Novelist John Steinbeck, who traveled with him in Russia to collaborate on a book, wrote in comic exaggeration: "Now Capa was out of his element, for Capa speaks all languages except Russian. He speaks each language with the accent of another. He talks Spanish with a Hungarian accent, French with a Spanish accent, German with a French accent, English with an accent that has never been identified. But Russian he does not speak. After a month he had picked up some words of Russian, with an accent which was generally considered Uzbek."

Like so many other intelligent boys of his time, André Friedmann was idealistic and impatient with the injustice he saw around him. In 1920, Hungary had become a dictatorship under Admiral Horthy. In 1930, at the age of seventeen, André joined young idealists opposing the dictator, just as he later would use his camera to record the evils of Fascism in Spain and Nazism all over the Continent. A concern for humanity, an acute awareness of its tribulations, developed early in him.

In 1931 he went to Berlin, where he intended to study sociology and journalism. ("Before I could learn the language enough to study anything," he wrote later, "I had no more money left to study at all.") For him the trip to Germany was the beginning of that perennial vagabondage which is the fate of all photojournalists. After Budapest he never had a conventional home again but moved from country to country, from hotel to hotel, living out of suitcases. At the age of eighteen he not only reached out, tentatively, for a career; he took the first step which would make him an internationalist.

In those days before Hitler the German capital was the cosmopolitan center for European intellectuals. Young André felt at home; while attending classes at the University of Berlin, he took a part-time job with

Ullstein Enterprises, a well-known group of magazines pioneering in the profession of photojournalism. His experience there is a perfect example of how a young laboratory assistant can become a photographer by grasping an opportunity when it arises. André's career as a working cameraman began one day, by chance, because nobody else was available to cover a speech in Copenhagen. He made the trip, and his photographs of Leon Trotsky were his first published work.

Soon after this André left Germany. Hitler had seized power and Berlin was no longer a pleasant place to live and work. The young photographer traveled to Vienna, where he stayed until early in 1933 when he journeyed to Budapest for a few months of picture-taking. Finally, in the fall of 1933, he went to Paris; there a legend began.

Now, legends often have basis in fact; but as a story passes from tongue to tongue, facts blend into fiction. Exaggeration sets in and truth, with all its fascination, is converted to legend. And legend requires a fabulous character whose feats grow with the passage of time. Here is a profile of the legendary Capa: *Gambler, a shark at poker* (actually, he was a poor card player) . . . *Lover of beautiful women* (true; women found him extremely attractive and he was a great success with them) . . . *Daring war correspondent* (he was indeed) . . . *Promoter* (he was a clever idea man, but no huckster) . . . *Cosmopolite* (the world was his studio and he was at ease wherever he went) . . . *Homeric drinker* (he drank no more, nor less, than most journalists) . . . *Historian and humanitarian* (he did leave a photographic legacy that shows the pernicious, demoralizing nature of war).

Fact and fiction lived side by side in this fascinating character whom novelist John Hersey called "The Man who invented himself." The invention took place in France in 1936. Poor and unknown, André Friedmann had to struggle to survive. Those were depression years and many talented people were in similar straits. André lived on the Left Bank of Paris; his girl friend was Gerda Taro, a beautiful blonde from Germany. Together they created a character named Robert Capa, a "rich, talented American photographer." André worked as a darkroom assistant and sales agent for this Capa. Soon the editors of French magazines were buying the photographs of this "talented American." Then the credit line "Photo by Robert Capa" began to appear in other European publications and, across the Atlantic, in *Time* magazine.

But one day André Friedmann went on assignment, posing as Capa. This was the final masquerade, for the young photographer was caught in his act by an editor who had been sold Capa photographs in his office and found Friedmann on the scene. André Friedmann died that very day and Robert Capa, full-grown and minus alias, was born. He was twenty-two, and fame was not far away.

Nearby, Spain was brewing a civil war between rebels and Loyalists. In France there was a strong pro-Loyalist feeling, which Capa shared; he decided to go and report what was really happening. Spain was a political arena, and a confusing one, in which the external forces of Russian Communism were dueling with German and Italian Fascism— and stepping on the Spanish dead in the process. The forces of totalitarianism were using Spain as a testing ground, trying out new weapons such as the Stuka dive-bomber, and training their officers for the bigger fight to come.

Democracy was being challenged, and men like Capa understood this. Writers and artists and intellectuals from all over the world poured into the country and gave not only their talents to the Loyalist cause but, in many cases, their lives as well. In the U. S., Ernest Hemingway raised thousands of dollars to buy ambulances, then crossed the ocean to serve as a correspondent and film-maker in the hope of alerting the world to the threat of Fascism. From this service came his fine novel *For Whom the Bell Tolls*. From the Spanish Civil War came Luis Quintanilla's Goyaesque sketchbook *All the Brave;* and other fine works, including Capa's first book, *Death in the Making*.

Spain was a crucible for Capa; there he had his first great success, and there he endured two searing experiences: the loss of a profound illusion and the loss of first love. His first sight of men dying must have shaken him. "When you go to war as a boy," Hemingway once wrote, "you have a great illusion of immortality. Other people get killed; not you." The horrible, bloody scenes of countrymen killing countrymen and devastating their fatherland quickly destroys any illusion a man has about being immortal.

Gerda Taro, his lovely girl friend, went with him to Spain in 1936.

During the battle of Brunete she was in the front lines and was crushed by a tank. No one can say with certainty what impact her death had upon Capa, for he did not discuss it much with his friends. But in 1938 he brought out *Death in the Making* (a photographic record of the Spanish Civil War), dedicating it "to Gerda Taro, who spent one year at the Spanish front, and who stayed on."

Gerda's tragic death and the terrible scenes he photographed made Capa hate war intensely. But the grim irony of the Spanish experience was that it also brought him international recognition. In Andalusia he took a picture that has become a classic. It caught a Loyalist soldier in the moment of death, toppling with a bullet in his head, one arm extended and his rifle trailing the ground. Capa shot the photograph from the top of a parapet, pressing the shutter release at the first sound of machine-gun fire. The legend of "close-up Capa" had begun—and with justification. Years later he would say, "If your pictures aren't good, you aren't close enough."

Men who have seen combat—soldiers and correspondents—had profound respect for his bravery and for his understanding of war. William Vandivert, a friend of Capa's and a war photographer himself, said that "Capa came to life in action. He was a great war photographer. Under stress he became like steel. He kept his head and knew what he was doing even though he was caught up in the event. And he believed that what he was doing was important, that he was serving in a just cause."

The late Brigadier General Theodore Roosevelt admired the photographer a great deal: "Capa," he said, "knows more about the art of war than many four-star generals." Another General, James Gavin, once said: "He was a good guy to have around. He had a lot of practical combat experience and he knew more about judging combat troops and how to fight than most of the so-called experts."

Spain matured Capa and prepared him—if anything ever can—for the wars he would record in the future. In January, 1938, he went to cover the fighting between China and Japan. There he recognized the universality of war: An air raid in Shanghai was as terrifying as an air raid in Madrid; a Chinese city burns as crisply as a Spanish city, and women weep in the ruins of all nations.

In China, Capa met a dauntless man who would become famous in   153

World War II. His name was Colonel Evans Carlson (of Carlson's Raiders), an American military observer. The Hungarian photographer followed the American officer on an eleven-day trek to Taierhchwang, where the Chinese won their only real victory of the war. Capa returned to Spain to film the final months of that civil war.

Then came World War II, and after France fell in 1940, Capa came to the United States to work for *Life*. (His father was dead and his mother and brother, Cornell,* now were living in America.)

In 1941, Capa was eager to return to Europe and cover the fighting, but his Hungarian citizenship made him an enemy alien and he was not permitted to leave America. However, *Collier's* magazine hired him as a correspondent and he managed to wangle his way out of the U. S. He crossed the Atlantic on a British warship and talked himself through English customs. (He was a persuasive man; he had to be, for his passport was a mere scrap of torn, dirty paper, stuck together with glue and tape!) But before he could see much action *Collier's* cabled its London office to recall him. This was an embarrassing development; without an assignment or correspondent's credentials he could be shipped back to the States as an enemy alien.

The now jobless enemy alien took evasive action—fleeing the city before the combined might of the Allied Public Relations Department could descend on him. Before leaving London he wired *Life* magazine, requesting a job and accreditation; then flew on to Algiers. There he met a photographer who had been scheduled to jump into Sicily with the 82nd Airborne. The man told a sad story; he had trained for months especially for the big mission, then got a bad case of diarrhea and had to confine himself to quarters—the men's room of the officer's club. Capa was solicitous, offering to take his place on the mission. How could this be done? He would need the permission of Major General Mathew Ridgeway, then commanding the 82nd. So the ingenious Hungarian hitched a ride on a plane, flew to an airfield in the middle of the Tunisian desert and was ushered into the office of Ridgeway.

---

* Cornell Capa also left Budapest after his graduation and joined his brother Bob in Paris. While Bob was in Spain, Cornell did all his lab work. Later in New York he took care of Bob's China material and their collaboration continued through the years. Somehow, Bob's pattern, with variations, was repeated and Cornell became a fine photographer, whose work has been appearing since 1946 in *Life* and other magazines.

"As long as you're willing to jump and take pictures of my division in combat," the general said, "I don't care whether you're Hungarian, Chinese, or anything else. Have you ever jumped before?"

"No, sir."

"Well, it isn't natural, but there's nothing to it."

Capa sat in the front of the big plane where he could take photos of the paratroopers as they jumped into the night. It had been decided that he shouldn't make this jump but should fly in the lead plane, photograph the first American to land in Sicily, then hurry back to radio the pictures to America. The boy sitting next to the photographer had been quiet for a long time, but finally couldn't resist asking:

"Is it true you're a civilian?"

"Yes."

The thought that Capa did not have to be there stunned the young paratrooper. Before bailing out he turned and yelled: "I don't like your job, pal. It's too dangerous."

The very next night Capa made his first jump into enemy territory. He had fallen asleep during the flight to the target area, and when the time came to bail out he had to be awakened! Stepping into the dark night and falling face forward, he recited groggily: "Fired photographer jumps." As the opening parachute jerked him backward he said: "Fired photographer floats." Three weeks later in Palermo the para-photographer met Ernie Pyle, who was arriving in the city with other correspondents. The skinny newsman hollered: "You blankety-blank fired enemy alien, the whole Public Relations is after you."

Of course, the bold Hungarian did not stay unemployed long; *Life* hired him again (he had worked for the magazine before and during the six-year stretch had been fired twice and quit once). He supplied pictorial reportage of the finest sort. "He took pictures which made you wonder how anyone could have photographed them and still be alive," correspondent Vincent Sheean said. Seventy-two hours after beachheads were established at Salerno, Capa was peering over the shoulders of infantrymen and clicking away.

Wherever he went he added to his stature as a combat cameraman. Writer Martha Gellhorn, a correspondent during World War II, recalls, "I had a perfect conviction that I would always meet Capa wherever it was blowing up, and always did; though we never had made any previous plans." He flew five missions in Flying Fortresses over Italy; he marched along with Darby's Rangers to Naples; he was one of the first correspondents to land at the Anzio beachhead.

The invasion of France saw Capa in the first wave to hit Omaha Beach. Following a tank ashore, bullets pinging its metal skin, shells plopping in the water, he repeated a saying from his Spanish days: *"Es una cosa muy seria. Es una cosa muy seria."* From this "serious business" came his powerful photo of a soldier in the surf, a photo that is a symbol of what Normandy means to a fighting man.

Late in 1944 he joined the 4th Armored Division, which was pushing toward Bastogne in an attempt to relieve the 101st Airborne trapped in the Belgian city. Capa was the only cameraman on this mission. Near Bastogne he climbed a hill and aimed his telephoto lens at a battalion of American infantry advancing over a snowy field. It would be an unusual photograph, he thought: soldiers (black figures), falling down and getting up (white background) under the gray puffs of exploding shells. About 150 yards away, a GI bellowed something at the photographer, at the same time raising his tommy gun.

"Take it easy! Capa hollered. Hearing the foreign intonation floating over the snow, the soldier opened fire, suspecting perhaps that the photographer was one of the English-speaking Germans who infiltrated American lines during the Battle of the Bulge. ("In *any* country," someone once said, "Capa talks and looks like an enemy alien.")

The quick-thinking Hungarian "surrendered," throwing up his arms and crying, "Kamerad!" Three trigger-happy men advanced to take him prisoner. When they got close enough to spot the expensive cameras Capa was carrying, joy burst out on their faces. They were about to "liberate" this equipment when the photographer asked them to "search my breast pocket."

One of the GIs studied the photographer's identification card and special pass signed by Dwight D. Eisenhower. A lugubrious look came over his face as the vision of the beautiful cameras vanished. "I should have shot him," he groaned.

156   Capa liked a good time; he was an entertaining companion. When

Ernest Hemingway arrived in London in 1944, Capa decided to throw a party for "Papa," who had befriended him through the years. Guests at the reùnion were the correspondents who were waiting for D-Day.

Capa was the caterer. He bought a fishbowl, a case of champagne, a bottle of brandy and six peaches. He soaked the peaches in the brandy, poured the champagne over them, and settled down to welcome his guests. It was a joyous reunion, and many friends of Hemingway crowded into the apartment. They were in a festive mood and celebrated with Homeric gusto. They finished the punch and polished off ten bottles of Scotch and eight bottles of gin. By 4:00 A. M. the fishbowl was dry, all the bottles empty, and the guests had trickled away. The caterer ate the peaches and went to sleep.

He was a charmer and women adored him. "When I first saw him I thought he was a gypsy," Rita Vandivert said, "with that wild hair and those flashing eyes. He was a romantic figure with a flair for drama —the kind of man who could enter a room wearing his coat like a cloak. He could carry off this kind of performance because it seemed natural for him. He would bowl in and out of the London office—I was working for the 'March of Time' then. When he arrived, warm and spontaneous, and asked to have some typing done, the girls all volunteered to help. They were devoted to him."

He showered women with attention, bought them presents, took them to the best places, loved them all—then left them. His women usually were bright and gentle and lovely creatures; he gave them affection, kindness and strength—while he was with them. And they returned it with love and loyalty. A Magnum photographer tells about the time he was returning from the Far East. The ship was crowded with evacuees; an American girl worked her way through the people to speak to him. She had heard that he was aboard and knew that he was a close friend of Capa. She introduced herself: "I'm one of Capa's girls," she said with great pride.

Mrs. Vincent Sheean knew him in Spain and later, during World War II, worked with him on a book project in London (*The Battle of Waterloo Road*). "My husband and I called him *Capita*—little Capa. He loved people and understood them completely. When we were doing the book, we talked to a lot of people in the Lambeth section. I remember this one family in particular—a wonderful old couple, the Gibbses, and their children. The entire family simply adored *Capita*—he was so natural with them, so deeply kind, absolutely straight and honest. It was marvelous what *Capita* could do with people; he could make them understand the way they were. He could have been a fine writer, you know. He had a great insight, a literary sense and a feeling for words. The book's concept and form were as much his as mine."

But photography was his life work and he was dedicated to it. Normally relaxed and gay, Capa became tense and waspish when he felt his work was threatened, as John Steinbeck noticed during their Russian tour: "The next morning it rained, and Capa feels that rain is a persecution of himself by the sky, for when it rains he cannot take pictures. He denounced the weather in dialect and in four or five languages. Capa is a worrier about films. There is not enough light, or there is too much light. The developing is wrong, the printing is wrong, the cameras are broken. He worries all the time. But when it rains, that is a personal insult addressed to him by the deity. He paced the room until I wanted to kill him, and finally went to have his hair cut, a real Ukranian pot haircut."

After World War II, Capa was out of a job, and happy not to be specializing in war photography. In 1947, he founded and became the first president of Magnum, the international photo agency. He was idea man, salesman and chief administrator for the new agency. He was also doing stories in Scandinavia and Europe for *Holiday* magazine and covering some assignments for *Life*. He toured Russia with John Steinbeck and made two trips to Israel (in 1948, to cover the war of liberation, and in 1950, when he collaborated on *Report on Israel* with Irwin Shaw).

By the early 1950s Capa was rather world-weary, slightly troubled, a little bored with his role of entrepreneur of Magnum Photos. He was rootless and lonely, with neither home nor children; and he suffered from a bad back which made working at photography painful. Thus he was happy to accept an offer in 1954 to go to Japan and give an exhibition of his photographs. It would be a pleasant change of pace, something of a holiday. Then *Life* asked him to go to the Indochina front and, like a trooper who cannot resist a bugle call, Capa swung into action.

When word flashed out of Indochina that Robert Capa was dead, people mourned in various parts of the globe. He had known many men and women, meeting them at bars and poker tables, at racetracks and on military missions; in the fields of Russia and Israel, in the editorial offices of Paris and New York. Steinbeck cabled a tribute from Paris:

"Capa has proved beyond all doubt that the camera need not be a cold mechanical device. Like the pen, it is as good as the man who uses it. . . . No one can take the place of any fine artist, but we are fortunate to have in his pictures the quality of the man. . . . He could photograph motion and gaiety and heartbreak. He could photograph thought. He made a world and it was Capa's world. . . ."

Hemingway wrote from Madrid: "He was a good friend and a great and very brave photographer. It is bad luck for everybody that the percentages caught up with him. It is especially bad for Capa. He was so much alive that it is a hard long day to think of him as dead."

To his friend, the great photographer Henri Cartier-Bresson, Capa was "a sort of magician, a man of tremendous generosity, intuitions, courage. And a gambler—a gambler in the sense that he was always challenging life, taking risks, in every respect."

Robert Capa was a true citizen of the world, the child of a violent century whose conscience tugged him to battle again and again. One of his last pictures shows a farmer in a field plowing; in the background a French Army convoy has been halted by a Viet Minh roadblock. The farmer pays no attention. This was the contrast—the peaceful peasant and the deadly war machine—he wanted for his photo essay. But there would be an unforeseen contrast that May afternoon:

Capa lying in a small field, a hole in his chest, one foot blown off. Side by side, beauty and death—the juxtaposition had happened before; at Shiloh men dropped among showers of peach blossoms that bullets scissored from the trees. Bob Capa died in the sun, near life-giving rice paddies and quick-growing plants.

Index